ADVAN

MW00715425

One in three women globally has been or will be abused in her lifetime. That's 1 billion women. And much of the abuse has been sexual. These adverse and common experiences often leave behind deep emotional wounds that prevent women from enjoying the fulfilling sex life that is their birthright and which contributes to overall health. In *How to Want Sex Again*, Alina Frank teaches you how to identify and release old sexual wounds using EFT (Tapping). I highly recommend her work.

CHRISTIANE NORTHRUP, M.D.
Author of the New York Times bestsellers: *Goddesses Never Age: The Secret Prescription for Radiance, Vitality, and Wellbeing, Women's Bodies, Women's Wisdom,* and *The Wisdom of Menopause*

With this generation's important sexual revolution underway—a revolution based upon self-knowledge, right relationship, power and pleasure rather than pain and shame, Alina Frank's new book HOW TO WANT SEX AGAIN comes at the right moment. Outlining the problems surrounding sexual intimacy in our culture, she provides a powerful antidote that leads to emotional freedom, EFT, through facing honestly and openly all our issues of self-doubt and fear of both loving and feeling worthy of love. I highly recommend this book to everyone—men and women—who would give anything to genuinely enjoy the pleasureful romp of sexual intimacy in their maturing relationships.

CAROLYN NORTH
Author of *ECSTATIC RELATIONS: A Memoir of Love*

Alina Frank has written a very well researched and easy to apply guide for using EFT for a very important topic. This book will help women everywhere begin the process of healing what has been for many a source of more pressure than joy.

CYNTHIA KERSEY
Best-selling author, *Unstoppable*

We are living in a world, where lasting, loving and healthy sexual relationships are more the exception than the rule. So many women and men enter permanent relationships already traumatized by hurtful and often violent sexual experiences. It is often up to the partner to offer help, but how can they do that without a background in healing and giving appropriate support? As an EFT Master trainer, I am grateful for Alina Frank's wonderfully insightful and gentle book which helps the reader heal those wounds and address sexual problems and trauma that are holding so many women and men back from enjoying a satisfying love life and fulfilling relationships.

INGRID DINTER
EFT Master Trainer and Coach

Alina Frank's book *How to Want Sex Again* is a treasure. Not only does she explain the technique of EFT Tapping, but she addresses an important and often ignored problem—the need to reignite the passion in women. As a psychotherapist for over 30 years, I hear women talk about their lack of sexual desire on an almost daily basis. I hear women repeatedly say that they feel obligated to "endure" sexual relations and often fake orgasms, so that the partner will end the act quickly and "they can get it over with. "This is a travesty and Alina's well-written book addresses topics like healing sexual abuse and affairs (from emotional to physical to online pornography), in a thoughtful and in-depth way. I cannot recommend this book highly enough and will be recommending it to patients, psychologists and physicians and other health providers.

ANNA RAYNE-LEVI, MA, LPCC
Integrated Behavioral Health Program Manager

EFT expert Alina Frank has written a remarkably helpful book about a very sensitive subject—how to increase sexual desire and satisfaction with our intimate partners. She compassionately engages the reader in exploring the myriad barriers that can lead to decreased passion, and then shows how Emotional Freedom Techniques can be used to heal the deeper causes, including past traumas, sexual abuse, health issues, infidelity, and low self-esteem.

This book is an EFT how-to manual applied to rekindling passion by tapping your own acupoints while describing how you feel about a specific problem or memory. It is designed for readers to use on their own, but she also delineates situations—e.g. when the emotional terrain is too uncomfortable to explore alone—where seeing an EFT practitioner may be helpful.

Written in a clear and friendly style, *How to Want Sex Again* features a variety of case studies that illustrate the successful use of EFT in this difficult and vulnerable arena. This book will change your life for the better. Highly recommended!

RICK INGRASCI M.D., M.P.H.
Co-author of the bestselling *Chop Wood, Carry Water: A Guide to Finding Spiritual Fulfillment in Everyday Life*

I highly recommend *How to Want Sex Again; Rekindling Passion with EFT* to anyone struggling with sexual and/or relationship challenges and to the practitioners treating these issues. A patient with a major infidelity breakdown synchronistically came to see me the week I started my review of this book, and thanks to Alina Frank's guidance, my EFT intervention was much more skillful resulting in a significant relationship breakthrough during the first tapping session. Alina's personal story and her client histories illustrate the principles of healing in a very effective fashion.

LARRY BURK, MD, CEHP
Author of *Let Magic Happen: Adventures in Healing with a Holistic Radiologist*

Whether you are a practitioner working in the field of sexual health, passionate about EFT or seeking your own sexual self-help guide, this is the must read book for you. Inspired by Alina Frank's own personal life experiences and packed with interesting case studies from thousands of clients, this book offers an honest, authentic and highly sensitive guide to rekindling your passion using EFT. So what are you waiting for? Grab this book and start tapping into a passionate new you.

ELIZABETH BOATH, PHD

This is an extraordinary book and likely to cause a revolution in healing, not only for sexual and relationship issues but for so many of the hidden causes of illness, pain, and unhappiness. Not only is it delightfully well-written and easy to follow, but it directly targets one of our primary "things least talked about and most hidden behind closed doors" with a gentle matter-of-factness and compassion that invoke courage for tackling the big issues and excitement for unleashing repressed libido. Prepare to watch for a surge of women's and men's creativity and empowerment following the publishing of Alina's new book.

LYNNAEA LUMBARD
Co-President, NewStories

Alina takes on one of the issues we don't like to talk about, and she does it with compassionate directness. You might want to say you are reading it for a friend, or you might want to simply start living the truth that we are all here to learn, and we are all here to heal. You can trust the awakening this book brings. It's all about love.

RABBI TED FALCON, PHD
Co-author of *Finding Peace Through Spiritual Practice.*

Alina Frank is far more than a wise and experienced healer. She rekindled her own passion with EFT and wants everyone to experience the joy and love her own life radiates. *How to Want Sex Again* skillfully demonstrates the path to joyful connection and opens the doorway to the healing and self-trust that women want to know is possible.

GAIL LARSEN
Author *Transformational Speaking: If You Want to Change the World, Tell a Better Story*

Alina's reputation as an international EFT trainer and practitioner as a specialist in the arena of women's sexuality comes through loud and clear with her compassion and desire to support and uplift women who have given away their power and their sexuality to others.

Good for you, Alina, for being brave enough to share your

own personal history as an example to others. You have given many women much needed hope.

SHARON CASS-TOOLE, PHD, DCEP, RP
President and Executive Director of C.A.I.E.T (The Canadian Association for Integrative and Energy Therapies)

This book is so much more than the title alludes to. Alina's experience as an EFT Trainer and Practitioner shines through the words in the book with references to her own story, case histories and her expertise in women's sexuality leading the reader confidently into an uplifting and healing way of being. This is a sensitive and much needed topic and Alina offers so much practical knowledge even to the seasoned practitioner. I'm recommending this book to all of my EFT students and practitioners as an essential resource they cannot afford to be without!

JENNY JOHNSTON
Best Selling Author of *Tapping into Past Lives,* Founder of Quantum EFT, International EFT Trainer and Practitioner

How To Want Sex Again is a brilliant, practical guide to embracing your passion. Alina Frank guides you step by step in how to identify and effectively release your limiting beliefs with EFT to achieve the intimacy, connection, and confidence you long for. Alina's expertise in women's sexuality comes through loud and clear with her compassion and desire to support and uplift women who have given away their power and their sexuality to others. A must read for women of all ages!

DALE PAULA TEPLITZ, M.A.
EFT Tapping Expert and Workshop Trainer

Drawing from her own past experiences, her many years as one of America's top energy Psychology Practitioners and from the sexuality workshops she runs with her husband Craig, Alina has become one of the foremost experts in understanding and resolving sexual issues preventing couples from experiencing loving, intimate relationships.

In this groundbreaking book *How to Want Sex Again: Rekindling Passion with EFT*, Alina's vast knowledge and understanding of this often taboo and overlooked subject shines through. By addressing areas of sexual dysfunction most practitioners shy away from, she has created a powerful resource for Energy Psychology Practitioners and lay people alike, enabling them to reconnect with their partners and create, loving, intimate relationships in place of awkwardness and embarrassment.

Pulling no punches, Alina explores the roots of sexual dysfunction from early childhood trauma to the creation negative beliefs around sex, and importantly offering powerful, effective tools to resolve these often unconscious blocks to sexual health.

Can you face your partner and openly say you have a perfect sexual relationship with them? If not then this is the book for you!!

KARL DAWSON
Creator of Matrix Reimprinting using EFT, Hay House Author

Thank goodness for Alina Frank! She has transformed a topic that is often filled with despair into a reason for deeper connection and true satisfaction. Do not wait a moment to dive into this clear, practical, and compassionate guide using well-tested EFT techniques to clear the way for a juicy sex life!

VICTORIA CASTLE
Embodiment Coach and author of *The Trance of Scarcity*

There are countless studies that reveal the health benefits of being in a healthy committed relationship. When you communicate with your body, it listens and your body will thank you for reading this book and respond in a positive way. In it, Alina Frank shows you how to use EFT to talk to your body in a way that will help you improve your relationships, so you can reap all the health-producing and life-prolonging benefits that it offers.

BERNIE SIEGEL, MD
Author of *Love, Animals & Miracles and The Art of Healing*

Alina brings a warm and engaging writing style as she addresses an essential human longing to be deeply seen and fully known. She provides an innovative approach to healing negative beliefs and emotional blocks that keep so many of us from experiencing the joy and contentment of sexual intimacy with our partner. I highly recommend Alina's book!

MIDGE MURPHY, JD, PHD (ENERGY MEDICINE)
Author *Practice Energy Healing in Integrity; the Joy of Offering Your Gifts Legally & Ethically*

YES! This book is so needed! FIND the cause, don't ignore—or worse yet—medicate it. Gracefully rich in story, resources and instruction, Alina's skill and expertise is clear and trustworthy. *How to Want to Have Sex Again: Rekindling Passion*, is a must read for anyone who desires experienced and comprehensive support for recreating passion in relationship and healing the wounds of intimacy.

TONI MARTHALLER-ANDERSEN, MSN, FNP-C
Integrative Nurse Practitioner at Women to Wellness and author of *Detox & Discovery*, a 6 week program to Healthier Living in Our Toxic Times.

As all my *Shameless* readers know, my entire life transformed when I reclaimed my sexuality and passion. Healing my past, learning to overcome a poor self-image of my body and overcoming my fears in order to embrace sex again has been the greatest gift I have ever given myself. Alina Frank, in this book, offers women a clear path to walk this journey. Every woman is entitled to become a sex goddess.

PAMELA MADSEN
Author of *Shameless: How I Ditched the Diet, Got Naked, Found True Pleasure...and Somehow Got Home in Time To Cook Dinner*

You truly have a gift in your hands with Alina's book *How to Want Sex Again: Rekindling Passion with EFT*. A leading, highly sought after and world trainer in EFT, Alina offers a comprehensive program in her book, which will change your intimate life for the better, and forever! This practical, how to guide busts apart what is really happening between the sheets and offers a way to get to the core of any issues quickly, and easily. The guide of how to use EFT (tapping) to mend and heal anything that is impacting your sex life is easy to follow and will result in transformational shifts in your beliefs, feelings and ultimately your sexuality. Every idea offered is backed with solid research and investigation, and the very real case vignettes presented allow every woman, everywhere on the planet to relate. The real message in this book is that all women have the right to feel joy as a sexual being and EFT is a phenomenal tool to allow that to become a reality.

DR. PETA STAPLETON
Clinical & Health Psychology and Leading World Researcher in EFT

Congratulations to Alina Frank for addressing the sensitive topic of sex in our intimate relationships in a respectful and sensitive manner. Alina also points out the importance of addressing our relationship with our own sexuality, self image and how we feel about our bodies. Written for a general audience, *How to Want Sex Again* describes a powerful tool—EFT—for resolving and improving these issues.

ANN ADAMS, LCSW
Author of *Effective Use of EFT*

On the basis of her years of clinical and personal experience, Alina Frank has written a remarkable and practical book that will prove of immense value to women, men, and their lovers. Sexless marriages and partnerships have become pandemic, and it is now time to administer very good medicine. Center stage: Alina's practical coaching and Emotional Freedom Techniques (EFT). Apply the advice and techniques offered here and you'll be absolutely astounded and grateful.

FRED P. GALLO PHD, DCEP
Author of *Energy Psychology* and President of the Association for Comprehensive Energy Psychology (ACEP).

We don't really protect ourselves by refusing to know ourselves, especially our sexual selves. In this comprehensive exploration, Emotional Freedom expert and trainer, Alina Frank offers up case studies and effective ways and means for making it safe to come to know our sexual selves in all its messy wonder and glory.

MARK BRADY, PH. D.
Author, *Fierce Listening*

A new *Joy of Sex* for the 21st Century, that helps smart couple root out deep seated barriers to meaningful and loving sex.

THORNTON WJA STREETER, DSC

Candid, comforting, competent. These are the ways I am familiar with the transformative EFT work that Alina Frank provides. Her book is delivered in the same clear manner as her EFT practice. If you want a different intimate experience, this is the book that will help you see your way.

MARY ANNE RADMACHER
Trainer and author of a dozen books

This indispensable book is about sex and so much more. Alina Frank has succeeded in addressing a bedrock issue in all relationships. She names some surprising facts and fears and correctly points out that sexual problems are about personal fears and beliefs that stop a person from being fully alive in his/her life. By focusing on these beliefs and fears that can lead to sexual problems, Frank gets to the heart of the matter. Through case studies and metaphors, she aptly allows the reader to easily understand how to use EFT on these issues. When self-help is not enough, she guides the reader to seek accessible professional EFT resources. Putting emotional safety first, Frank has triumphed in bringing the world a comprehensive manual for clearing sexual issues once and for all. This book is a straightforward read that flows through techniques, stories and sexual truths leaving the reader ready to want to have sex again.

SUZANNE FAGEOL, MDIV, MSD
Certified Counselor, Somatic Trauma Educator

Alina Frank skillfully explains how to apply key principles of classical EFT—using gentle curiosity to be specific, being non-judgmental and promoting acceptance of self and others—thus providing a much needed route to escape the effects of past hurts and fears, which will help so many move forward with relationships. Alina not only knowledgeably addresses an under-resourced topic that some may find difficult to tackle, but does so in a clear, well-illustrated, honest, practical and empowering way that is eminently readable and usable. A great addition to the fast-growing body of EFT self-help literature, but also valuable information for serious students of EFT.

JACQUI FOOTMAN
EFT Trainer/Practitioner, Chair, AAMET, International not-for-profit Professional EFT Association

Through her candid willingness to create a space of openness and trust, Alina Frank guides us to explore and heal what most of us want to keep secret—our sex life! From a lackluster sex life, childhood sexual trauma, to discussing sex with teens, her well-researched workbook-style guide takes us step by step through the process of inner work that can lead us to, as the title says, want sex again and rekindle our passion.

Alina's approachable and warm style make it feel "okay" to talk about commonly taboo topics—it's no surprise that she is an internationally recognized EFT specialist on women's sexuality and has served as a counted on EFT coach for thousands of clients.

Let Alina be your trusted guide as you take the time to tend to a healthy, fulfilled sex life, and then get busy rekindling passions throughout all areas of your life!

CHRISTY KORROW
Editor, Lilipoh Magazine

Alina Frank has created a safe container to address the deep and varied issues that underlie lost sexual desire.

Her clarity and compassion make passage through vulnerable experiences navigable. *How to Want Sex Again* is an empowering guide and an invaluable asset to anyone seeking healing and real-life shifts.

ELIZABETH FREDIANI
Author of *Where Body Meets Soul: Subtle Energy Healing Practices for Physical and Spiritual Self-Care*

Direct, simple, honest and powerful, Alina Frank's book is a shortcut to letting go of the most common barriers to great sex. Packed with moving case histories and clear examples, it shows how to apply the wildly popular Emotional Freedom Techniques method to create a rich and satisfying sex life. It shows how emotions, especially traumatic childhood experiences, can prevent us from experiencing pleasure and connection with our partners. Practical and brief sections show how to create healthy boundaries, approach painful past experiences that limit our present possibilities, cultivate a sense of playfulness, and awaken the parts of our brains that respond to intimate connection. This is a book for anyone seeking to reclaim the sensual enjoyment that is our natural human birthright.

DAWSON CHURCH, PHD, CEHP
Author of *EFT for Love Relationships*

An insightful and well-written guide to help women restore intimacy in their lives and reawaken the sexual self. Thoughtful and uplifting, this book contains helpful advice and practical techniques to help women gain freedom from emotional barriers which may be preventing them from having an active and enjoyable sex life, whether from painful past experiences or society's negative programming. It offers a practical guide to how women can use EFT tapping to become free to explore their sexual nature without the pressure of fear, false expectations, or guilt. Those who read it and apply its advice can look forward to happier and more fulfilled relationships.

STEVE WELLS
Psychologist

HOW TO WANT SEX AGAIN

Rekindling Passion
Using EFT

BY ALINA FRANK

Contributing Writer: Petra Martin

Cover Design: John Matthews

Interior Book Design: Heidi Miller

Editing: Kate Makled & Adrienne Sharpe

Author's Photo Courtesy of: Linda Schwarz

Dedication

To my beloved soulmate-earthmate, Craig, who has shown me passion and intimacy beyond my wildest dreams.

DISCLAIMER

Please read the following before proceeding further.

The information presented in this book, titled *How to Want Sex Again: Rekindling Passion Using EFT*, ("Book"), including ideas, suggestions, exercises, techniques, and other materials, is educational in nature and is provided only as general information. This Book is solely intended for the reader's own self-improvement and is not meant to be a substitute for medical or psychological treatment and does not replace the services of health care professionals.

This Book contains information regarding an innovative healing technique called Emotional Freedom Techniques or EFT. EFT looks at and seeks to address stressors and imbalances within a person's energy system, as well as the energetic influence of thoughts, beliefs, and emotions on the body. EFT is based on ancient Chinese acupuncture and balances an individual's energy with a gentle tapping procedure that stimulates designated acupoints on the face and body while focusing on issues of emotional intensity in order to release the intensity and reframe the issues. The prevailing premise of EFT is that the flow and balance of the body's electromagnetic and more subtle energies are important for physical, spiritual, and emotional health, and for fostering well-being.

Although EFT appears to have promising emotional, spiritual, and physical health benefits, and there is a growing amount of scientific research indicating that EFT is an effective evidence-supported technique—especially for managing stress—EFT has yet to be fully researched by the Western academic, medical, and psychological communities. Therefore, EFT may be considered experimental. The reader agrees to assume and accept full responsibility for any and all risks associated with reading this Book and using EFT. If the reader inadvertently experiences any emotional distress or physical discomfort using EFT, the reader is advised to stop and to seek professional care, if appropriate.

Publishing of the information contained in this Book is not intended to create a client-practitioner or any other type of professional relationship between the reader and the author. While the author is an experienced EFT practitioner and trainer, the author is not a licensed health care provider. The author does not make any warranty, guarantee, or prediction regarding the outcome of an individual using EFT for any particular purpose or issue.

By continuing to read this Book, the reader agrees to forever, fully release, indemnify, and hold harmless, the author, and others associated with the publication of this Book from any claim or liability and for any damage or injury of whatsoever kind or nature that the reader may incur arising at any time out of, or in relation to, the reader's use of the information presented in this Book. If any court of law rules that any part of the Disclaimer is invalid, the Disclaimer stands as if those parts were struck out.

By continuing to read the book you agree to all of the above.

TABLE OF CONTENTS

Foreword

Introduction

How to tell if this book is for you

What lies ahead

A few notes

    How to read this book

    Nouns, pronouns, and assumptions

    Case studies

1

Chapter 1
MY WAKE-UP CALL

5

Chapter 2
HOTDOGS OR HAMBURGERS?

    Identifying your own needs

    Speaking your needs

    Learning to love the body you're in

    Identifying delights, edges, and boundaries

17

Chapter 3

TAKING MATTERS INTO YOUR OWN HANDS

Ten reasons to self-pleasure and two reasons not to

When self-pleasuring can make things better

When self-pleasuring can make things worse

27

Chapter 4

WHAT EFT IS AND HOW IT WORKS

1. A specific event or condition

2. The emotion(s) you feel in response to that event or condition

3. The origin, location, or source of that emotion in the body

4. Self-acceptance

5. Tapping acupoints

35

Chapter 5

BEFORE YOU BEGIN—PAVING THE WAY FOR HEALING

Addressing fears that may prevent you from healing

Outsmarting your subconscious mind

When to work with an EFT practitioner

49

Chapter 6

A FEW OF YOUR FAVORITE THINGS

Outer resources

Inner resources

55

Chapter 7

WAIT. HOW DID I GET HERE?

Identifying "tappable" issues

Little stimulus, big response

Limiting issues

What to do if tapping takes you somewhere unexpected

61

Chapter 8

HOW TO TAP—LEARNING THE BASICS

A precaution

Overview

1. Creating the setup statement

2. Creating the reminder phrase

3. Tapping

4. Re-rating and repeating

Download the journal template

What to say when you do EFT

Creating your setup statement

What to do while you're saying your setup statement and reminder phrase

The acupoints

Tapping FAQ

How quickly should I tap?

How often should I tap each point?

How much pressure should I use?

How important is it to tap the exact location of the acupoint?

Does it matter which eye I tap or which arm I tap under?

Does it matter which hand I use?

How many fingers should I use?

What if my eyeglasses are in the way? I can't read these directions without them.

Why state these problems negatively? Doesn't that go against the law of attraction or positive thinking?

Practice tapping

Putting it all together

Circle back

79

Chapter 9:
CREATING A SAFETY NET WITH EFT

83

Chapter 10:

OUCH! OVERCOMING PHYSICAL PAIN OR DISCOMFORT

Preparing to tap

Where's the pain?

What size is the pain?

What's the quality of the pain?

How intense is the pain?

Tapping to relieve pain

Creating your setup statement

The reminder phrase

Putting it all together and tapping

Re-rate the intensity

What to do if the pain doesn't abate

Symptoms as metaphors

95

Chapter 11:

HEALING YOUR HEART—OVERCOMING EMOTIONAL PAIN

Start where you are

The root of pain and discomfort

101

Chapter 12:
EMOTIONAL SPRING CLEANING

The Personal Peace Procedure

Step 1: Make your list

Step 2: Assess the intensity of each item in your list

Step 3: Tap on one or two items on your list every day

If you can't get the intensity level down to zero or low

A word of caution

111

Chapter 13:
THE POWER OF BELIEF

When solitude seems life-threatening

When men seem dangerous

What are your limiting beliefs?

Clearing limiting beliefs with EFT

Tabletops and table legs

If you need help

121

Chapter 14:
THE MIND-BODY CONNECTION

When did it start?

What was happening in your life six months to a year before it started?

What could this be a metaphor for?

If your body was sending you a message, what might it be saying?

What is your physical condition saying (to yourself or others) that you couldn't say yourself?

How do you feel about your condition? What else do you feel that way about?

What makes your condition better? What makes it worse?

The body remembers

Theresa, Thomas, and cold fish

Helping your body reveal its secrets

131

Chapter 15:
WHAT'S THE PAST GOT TO DO WITH IT?

When smoke alarms go off too often

The impact of adverse childhood experiences (ACEs)

141

Chapter 16:
HEALING THE ULTIMATE BETRAYAL

Primary betrayal

Secondary betrayal

EFT offers a path to healing, but do not travel alone

149

Chapter 17:
RECOVERING FROM ABANDONMENT AND NEGLECT

Neglect

The hedgehog's dilemma

155

Chapter 18:
EFT AND YOUR RELATIONSHIP

Money

Parenthood

Physical issues

Distractions

Reestablishing connection

167

Chapter 19:
HEALING THE SEXLESS MARRIAGE

171

Chapter 20:
OVERCOMING THE PAIN OF INFIDELITY

Rebuilding trust

The fork in the road

Infidelity prevention

177

Chapter 21:
WHEN "AFFAIRS" AREN'T PHYSICAL

Digital infidelity

Emotional infidelity

185

Chapter 22:
YOUR TAPPING TROUBLESHOOTER

Are you being specific?

Are you tapping on something positive instead of
something negative?

Are you scoring emotional intensity?

Are you documenting your experiences?

Have you addressed underlying medical issues?

Is there a hidden benefit that prevents you from letting
go of the problem?

Are you dehydrated?

Are you able to see your own problem objectively?

195

Chapter 23:
GO FORTH AND HEAL

197

Works Cited

205

Acknowledgements

207

About the Author

FOREWORD

One of the world's foremost sex therapists, David Schnarch, is fond of telling new clients whose passion has gone out of their marriage that sexual desire problems are normal, that they mean "everything's happening as it should!" This news is, however, probably of little consolation to the estimated 20 million couples in the U.S. who are living with what psychiatrists call "hypoactive sexual desire" and do not have the privilege of being in therapy with Dr. Schnarch.

For that group, another source of hope and effective guidance is available, and you are holding it in your hands. Its author, Alina Frank, has known sexual desire from both sides. Passion in her first marriage faded into oblivion, sexless in its final decade, with Alina coming to believe that she was "one of those women who just didn't want sex." Now in her fifties and in a fulfilling marriage, she is more sexually active than at any previous time in her life. In addition to sex being marvelously enjoyable and an essential ingredient in her deep bond with her husband, she reflects that "I know now that sex can be energizing when I'm tired, can get rid of a headache, and can make me feel calm and relaxed when I'm feeling stressed." Beyond these personal credentials, Alina has helped thousands of individuals and couples regain their passion as they cultivated the "universal longing for intimacy, for soulful connection, and unconditional love."

What makes this book rise above what Schnarch and a hundred other resources on rekindling passion have to offer is that, in addition to being attuned to contemporary scientific knowledge and breakthroughs in sex therapy, it teaches the reader physical techniques for shifting the energies that inhibit sexual desire, connection, and fulfillment. One of the most important breakthroughs of recent decades in psychotherapy and self-guided personal development is that stimulating acupuncture points by tapping on them can change the way the brain processes information, transforming outmoded beliefs and creating new emotional patterns. Alina has been brilliant in her application of this method (using a form of it called the "Emotional Freedom Techniques," or simply "EFT") in her clinical work, and she has managed to chunk down the many complex aspects of sexuality into bite-sized pieces, with each clearly addressed in the book's 23 brief chapters.

If we had to select one word to describe the book's probable effect on the reader, that word would be "empowering." You quickly learn that your sexuality is intimately connected with many other issues in your life, from how you feel about your body to how deeply you can connect with another person. You are then provided with expert guidance on how to apply EFT to navigate your way through every micro-stumbling block and every major issue you are likely to encounter in expanding yourself into a more joyfully loving partner.

How to Want Sex Again can be read by those who want to rekindle passion in their relationship, but it also holds many gems for single people who long for a deeply gratifying partnership. For couples, it is often the less satisfied partner who will be drawn to a book like this. That is a great starting point, but as you delve into the book's guidance and start to derive some of its benefits, share your experiences with your partner. That's all. Put no pressure on your partner to use EFT. Your partner is, however, likely to become interested. Use that interest to build a bridge between what exists between you and what is possible.

The answers are not simple, and the steps toward deeper love and passion have not been charted for your unique relationship, but the guidance provided in this book can be invaluable for helping you find your way.

DONNA EDEN AND DAVID FEINSTEIN, PH. D.
October 2015 | Ashland, Oregon

INTRODUCTION

Have you ever struggled with a problem for a long time, finally found a solution, and then felt like shouting it from the housetops so others wouldn't have to go through what you did? That's what happened to me, and this book is my "shout."

Since I found my solution, I've seen it help thousands of clients and students. But helping them one-on-one doesn't help *you*, and I've been thinking about you for a long time. The best way to reach you was to write a book, and I'm so glad we finally found each other.

How to tell if this book is for you

This book can help if:

- You yearn for the closeness that you once shared with your partner, but therapy, self-help books, and other attempts at reconnecting have failed.

- You feel unattractive and less comfortable in your body because of the way it changed after you carried and gave birth to a child.

- You're too uncomfortable with your own sexuality to handle the budding sexuality of your pre-teens or teens.

- You fear that your disinterest in sex may have driven your partner to Internet porn, or a physical or emotional affair.

- You find that sex is something you endure, if you can't avoid it altogether.

- You have health issues that prevent you from having sex.

The solution I learned about is Emotional Freedom Techniques (EFT), and I've seen it successfully address all of these problems time and time again. It's easy to learn and highly efficient: you can sometimes clear an issue in a single session. EFT is inexpensive and completely private because, in most cases, you don't have to see or pay a professional practitioner. (To help you determine whether you need a practitioner, see the section titled "When to work with an EFT practitioner" in Chapter 5.)

This book, along with supporting materials on my website, will teach you how to use EFT on your own to achieve the intimacy, connection, and confidence you long for. But just reading it won't change your life. Doing EFT will achieve that. Before you continue reading, commit yourself to applying what you learn in this book. You have nothing to lose, and so much to gain!

What lies ahead

Here's what you'll find in the pages ahead:

- Chapter 1 is about how my kids' looming adolescence forced me to deal with my sexless marriage–and how EFT rebooted my life.

- Chapter 2 is about identifying what your own needs are, speaking those needs, and learning to love the body you're in.

- Chapter 3 is about getting to know your body better and learning what feels pleasurable to you.

- Chapter 4 explains what EFT is and how it works.

- Chapter 5 helps you identify fears and hidden benefits that may be preventing you from healing.

- Chapter 6 is about your resources–things that bring you to a state of integration and wholeness.

- Chapter 7 helps you to identify which issues you can use EFT on.

- Chapter 8 teaches you how to do EFT step by step (but please read your way up to that chapter–don't skip right to it).

- Chapter 9 is about a useful EFT technique that you can use anytime you're feeling overwhelmed and need help getting grounded in the present moment.

- Chapter 10 helps you overcome physical pain and discomfort using EFT.

- Chapter 11 is about relieving painful emotions using EFT.

- Chapter 12 helps you create an inventory of all the painful experiences you've had in your life, so you can heal each one using EFT.

- Chapter 13 addresses the painful thoughts or beliefs that may have been holding you back and teaches you how to use EFT to clear them.

- Chapter 14 is about what your body knows and how it tries to communicate with you.

- Chapter 15 connects past adverse experiences to the present and teaches you how to break their hold on you.

- Chapter 16 is about healing childhood sexual abuse, including the pain caused by abusers and by those who looked the other way or disbelieved you.

- Chapter 17 is about healing childhood abandonment and neglect—the failure of caregivers to meet basic human needs.

- Chapter 18 covers the most common sources of conflict in partnered relationships, such as money and childrearing.

- Chapter 19 is about the startling number of marriages that become sexless–including my first one.

- Chapter 20 is about healing the pain of infidelity, so you can repair your relationship or move on without baggage.

- Chapter 21 is about "non-physical" infidelity, including use of Internet porn and emotional affairs.

- Chapter 22 contains some tips and tricks to try if EFT isn't working for you.

- Chapter 23 is my parting wish for you.

I'm confident that EFT can help you want sex again. This book will show you how to get there, and I look forward to walking with you on this journey.

A few notes

HOW TO READ THIS BOOK

To establish a solid foundation for your EFT practice, and to ensure your comfort and safety, please read Chapters 1 through 9 of this book *in order*. After that, feel free to skip to the chapters that most interest you.

NOUNS, PRONOUNS, AND ASSUMPTIONS

EFT is a universal healing technique that works for both men and women. That said, I had to make some assumptions and decisions when I wrote this book. Most of my clients are heterosexual women who want to improve their relationships with male partners. EFT has worked for them, but it works just as well for men in relationships with women or people of either gender in relationships with partners of the same sex. For the sake of readability, I wrote this book assuming a female reader working to improve her relationship with a male partner. If that's not the case for you, the procedures in this book will work equally well, and I apologize if my decision to use hetero-normative language leaves you feeling excluded in any way. That was not my intention, and I look forward to the day when the English language offers us pronouns that make everyone feel included.

CASE STUDIES

The case studies in this book are true, but I've changed names and identifying details to protect the privacy of those involved.

CHAPTER 1
MY WAKE-UP CALL

I didn't realize until I was in my forties that I'd handed the reins of my sexual wellbeing over to the men in my life. If they wanted sex, I had it. If they didn't, I didn't. In my first marriage, lingerie, privacy, and lots of time to ourselves quickly gave way to sweat pants, staying up with a teething toddler, and an ear that was always attuned to the cry of a child.

Soon, sex took place only on anniversaries, birthdays, and vacations. Alcohol, which had made us more relaxed in the beginning, became essential to take the edge off the awkwardness and sense of obligation. Then one day, our sex life fell asleep and never woke up again.

I became a doula (someone who assists women during, and sometimes after, childbirth), and then, in 2006, I learned EFT (Emotional Freedom Techniques). My first clients tended to be people who were struggling with infertility, and when I asked them "How's your sex life?" the answer was always the same: "Pitiful," "Nonexistent," and "What sex life?" EFT helped resolve the issues that prevented these couples from enjoying physical intimacy and often helped them conceive the baby they longed for.

At some point, I had to ask myself the same question that I asked my clients: "How's *my* sex life?" My answers were the same as theirs, and I knew I didn't want to be a do-as-I-say-not-as-I-do type of EFT practitioner. By then, my husband and I hadn't had sex for ten years. I realized that it wasn't possible for me to be fully human if I wasn't fully embodied, and I couldn't be fully embodied if I wasn't having the most intimate physical experience that two people can share. I didn't want a roommate. I wanted a romantic partner.

The fact that my children's puberty was looming on the horizon filled me with a sense of urgency. I knew I couldn't help them navigate the waters of their own adolescence if I couldn't talk to them about sex in an authentic way. Something had to be done, and I had to be the one to do it.

My children's father and I divorced, and I've since remarried. Now, when my husband looks at pictures of me that were taken during the last ten years of my first marriage, he says, "I don't even recognize you." There's a vitality that's missing in those pictures. Once I started making love again, my senses awoke, my creativity surged, and my appearance changed.

Now, I accept myself in a way that I never have before. My husband's delight in me, regardless of my weight, shows my kids that neither they nor their partners have to measure up to someone else's photoshopped ideal to be worthy of love.

I can tell my kids from personal experience that sex is enjoyable and can lead to greater connection and intimacy. They know that my own healing led me to help others heal–particularly around relationships and sex. Thanks to what I've learned from my clients, I encourage my kids to trust their intuition, have safe sex, make sure they get consent, and use birth control. Most of all, my healing prevents them from inheriting my emotional baggage. I know that sex is part of a happy and fulfilled life, and I want that for them.

Many of my clients *say* they want more intimacy with their partners. They've tried to achieve it through talk therapy, self-help books, medication, date nights, and weekends away. But when I probe further, it turns out that they avoid sex in many conscious and unconscious ways. Some have headaches or painful periods (or say they do when they don't). Some make sure their partner goes to sleep before they do by working late, surfing the Internet, using social media, or watching television. Some become helicopter moms and use over-involvement with their children as an excuse not to be with their mates. Some gain weight and make themselves less physically desirable, or they become perfectionists who won't make love unless countless criteria are met.

The ironic thing is that they don't hate their partners. They long for more intimacy and connection–they'd just prefer to achieve it without having to have sex. In my experience, and in the experience of hundreds of my clients, that isn't possible. Emotional and sexual intimacy are inseparable in a relationship. Intimacy of any kind requires vulnerability, which author Brené Brown is helping us all to see in a more positive light. She says, "We cultivate love when we allow our most vulnerable and powerful selves to be deeply seen and known."

That's what this book is about: helping you achieve the intimacy you seek by making it safe to be deeply seen and fully known. I know it takes courage to be vulnerable, but you're not alone. I'll be on this journey with you, and I have a perspective that you don't: I've seen EFT work for thousands of clients, and I'm confident that it can work for you.

CHAPTER 2
HOTDOGS OR HAMBURGERS?

"I shouldn't have to ask him for what I need," my client said. "If he loved me, he'd *know*."

"Do *you* know what you need?" I asked. She sputtered.

"If *you* don't know, is it fair to expect *him* to?"

Her eyes widened, "Good point," she said. "How do I figure that out?"

Identifying your own needs

We tend to give love in the way that we prefer to receive it. Say Chicago-style hotdogs make your partner feel loved and cheeseburgers make you feel loved. He gives you hotdogs, but you hate them. Does he love you? Of course he does. Do you feel loved? *No.*

Here's what's going on in his mind: "Chicago-style hot dogs rule! I always had one when I went to Cubs games with my dad. Eating one brings back such great memories. I want to share that feeling with my beloved."

Here's what's going on in your mind: "I hate hot dogs! Why doesn't he get that? Cheeseburgers remind me of the A&W drive-in we used to go to on Sundays when I was a kid. The kind where they brought the food out to your car. My sister and I used to love that."

Say you actually reach the point where you *get* that he likes Chicago-style hot dogs and he *gets* that you like cheeseburgers. Do you just jump straight to providing each other with the foods you love? Probably not. First, you'll try to convince him that he's wrong. Maybe he just hasn't had the right *kind* of cheeseburger, you think. You begin checking out different burger places around town in an effort to convert him. Because, wouldn't it be great if you *both liked cheeseburgers*?

What we have here is two people who love each other but express love in different ways, resulting in neither one of them feeling loved. Like archers, they aim love at their partners, but miss the target every time. Psychologist Gary Chapman has come up with a way to resolve this problem by helping people identify their "love language." There are five languages, including:

- Words of affirmation

- Acts of service

- Receiving gifts

- Quality time

- Physical touch

If your primary love language is acts of service, all the I-love-yous in the world aren't going to make you feel loved–but changing the oil in your car might. If his primary love language is quality time, a truckload of gifts isn't going to make him feel loved—but a date might. (Chapman)

To learn what your own love language is, go to 5lovelanguages.com, and take the quiz.

Here's an example of how learning her love language helped one of my clients. Harriet was woman in her early fifties who came to work with me on her relationship issues. I started with all the usual questions:

"How do you know something is wrong?"

"When do you think this started?"

"How does this situation remind you of previous relationships?"

I also asked how her sex life was. She said that she'd given up on sex years before and noted that no one had ever asked her that question before. I find that remarkable.

I asked Harriet if she knew what her love language was. She said she had *The 5 Love Languages* book on her shelf, but had never read it or taken the quiz. I felt it was a perfect place to start and invited her to share her discovery process with Tim, her husband of 25 years. Tim took the quiz online, and Harriet, who read the book, took the quiz printed there. A week later, Harriet said she'd discovered that receiving gifts was her primary love language. For people like Harriet, giving and receiving gifts isn't just caving in to consumer culture. They share love by giving or receiving things as simple as a wild flower picked on the side of the road or a beautiful feather found on a trail.

Tim had discovered that his primary love language was physical touch. He felt loved when Harriet touched him and expressed his love by touching her. This expression can look as simple as a hug when you come home in the evening, receiving a foot massage, or holding hands. It can also mean sex, and this turned out to be a major part of their relationship conflict.

Harriet realized that she had distanced herself from her husband because she'd misinterpreted his need for any kind of touch as initiating sex. She interpreted a simple hug as a sexual advance. This led Harriet to remember past sexual trauma that contributed to her lack of interest in sex with Tim. We used EFT to decrease the emotional intensity around those memories.

When Harriet learned to differentiate between simple physical connection and sexual foreplay, it made a huge impact on the quality of her relationship with Tim. In turn, Tim found ways to show his love for Harriet by bringing home flowers unexpectedly or buying her a small trinket when he traveled on business.

Harriet achieved her goal of resolving her relationship issues, but it all started with Harriet identifying what her love language was. Communicating that to Tim empowered him to make gestures that hit the target and made Harriet feel loved. Knowing Tim's love language helped Harriet understand that he'd been trying to express love for decades and also empowered her to make gestures that made him feel loved. Win win.

When partners don't speak each other's love language, it puts their relationship at risk. My friend Elisabeth was married to a man who didn't speak her love language, which was acts of service, closely followed by receiving gifts. When her husband's friend came to visit from Europe, he carried her groceries, opened doors for her, and gave her a parting gift that was based directly on a conversation they'd had. Sometime later, a dear male colleague brought Elisabeth some bay leaves that he'd harvested over the weekend. These simple gestures moved her to tears and made her feel more loved than her husband did. Fortunately, both men were gay, but what if they hadn't been? How many affairs begin when a thoughtful gesture is mistaken for love, just because it hit the mark?

Speaking your needs

If your love language is gifts, is there a special kind of gift you prefer, and is there a time when receiving it would be most appreciated? This information can provide your partner with the if/then scenario that sets him up for success. "If I get bad news, then getting flowers cheers me up." "If I have a bad day at work, then picking up a pizza on your way home prevents me from having to think about what's for dinner and gives me more time to unwind." "If I have a cold, then bringing me orange juice and chicken soup makes me feel better."

Knowing what your needs are is the first step. Asking your partner to meet those needs is the second, and that's where many people run into trouble. Their feelings range from:

- **Angry** that they have to express their needs at all.

- **Afraid** that their partner might refuse to meet their needs.

- **Vulnerable** because they don't want to feel dependent on or indebted to someone else for meeting their needs.

- **Trusting** that their partners would want to meet their needs once they know what they are.

- **Empowered** by the self-knowledge that enables them to communicate their needs.

- **Relieved** that knowing and communicating their needs may help them solve their problems.

If the thought of sharing your love language with your partner evokes negative emotions, you can use EFT to decrease their intensity. Continue to read this book until you get to Chapter 8, and then circle back here to address the issues that prevent you from sharing your needs with your partner.

After you've reduced the intensity of the negative emotions that prevent you from speaking your needs, you can ask yourself questions like these, and use EFT on any memories that arise:

- "Where did I learn to fear expressing my needs?"

- "When, in the past, has someone not responded favorably when I expressed my needs or desires?"

Learning to love the body you're in

Emily Nagoski, author of *Come as You Are: The Surprising New Science that Will Transform Your Sex Life* says, "Negative body image is among the most common causes of sexual dysfunction. But more than that, it's manufactured misery that generates profits for corporations at the expense of women's power in the world. It cripples us and keeps us in chains." (Nagoski, 2011)

Nagoski encourages us to "follow the money." Who profits when you hate yourself? The U.S. diet industry is valued at nearly $60 billion dollars per year. (Marketdata-Enterprises, 2015) The U.S.cosmetics market is valued at more than $60 billion dollars annually (Statista), and the cosmetic surgery market is valued at $12 billion dollars. (ASAPS, 2014) That's more than $413 a year for every man, woman, and child in the U.S.

Of course, realizing that a number of industries have a vested interest in your poor body image doesn't suddenly make you love yourself. That takes time; but awareness and EFT can help you achieve it. My client Marla's experience is an example. Marla made an appointment to work on her extreme self-loathing. She said it affected every part of her life, from feeling uncomfortable in social situations, to being unable to ask for a raise, to feeling insecure about her sexuality. She'd read that loving herself was the key to happiness in a number of self-help books, but that only made her angry.

In my experience, people look in the mirror in two ways. They either focus on what needs to be done (such as flossing their teeth or putting in contacts) and avoid the things they hate, or they zero in on the things they hate and focus only on those. Marla's was an extreme case of the latter. When I asked her how she felt when she looked in the mirror, she said, "I hate every part of myself."

"Isn't there one thing that you like or love?" I asked.

"I don't love anything," she said. But after a moment of deep thought she added, "Well there's a dimple on my right cheek that I like."

We had our work cut out for us! Over the following months, Marla continued to see me, and her homework assignments began with her doing EFT at home on each thing that she hated about her face. When she felt neutral about her face, her assignment was to look in a full-length mirror and do EFT on each hated area of her fully clothed body. When no part of her clothed body evoked hatred, her assignment was to stand in front of a full-length mirror naked, and again do EFT for every loathed body part.

During the course of our work together, Marla went from avoiding mirrors, to feeling neutral about looking at herself, to finding that there were parts of her body that she really enjoyed. This simple, yet profound process transformed Marla's life. A byproduct of her work was that she lost weight, but for her, the greatest change was in her ability to confidently move about the world with her head held high.

I recommend the mirror exercise to clients during and after transitions: as women's bodies grow larger and feel more foreign during pregnancy; after they've given birth; after body-altering surgery, such as a mastectomy; and after menopause. We never seem to finish learning to love our bodies. We have to learn to love them over and over again, and EFT can help. Continue to read this book until you get to Chapter 8, and then circle back here to address any issues that prevent you from loving your body just as it is.

After EFT has neutralized any feelings of self-loathing that you have for your body, ask yourself questions like these, and use EFT on any memories that arise:

- "Where did I learn to hate my body?"

- "Where did I learn to be afraid that others might reject me based solely on my appearance?"

- "When did being myself first feel unsafe?"

Identifying delights, edges, and boundaries

Another thing that can help you know yourself is to identify what delights you and determine where your edges and boundaries are.

- Delights are the things that make you purr; the things that make you lose control, gasp, or moan with pleasure.

- Edges are things that you want to do, but don't have the nerve to do. For example, making love in nature, where there's a slight risk of being seen (or winding up in satellite view on Google Maps). You can use EFT to help give you courage to get closer to your edges.

- A boundary is something that goes against your values. It's something you don't want to do, and the only reason you'd do it is to please someone else. For example, participating in a threesome might be outside your boundary. You should never violate your own boundaries. (Note that people who have been sexually abused often have no boundaries because theirs were so often violated. In cases like these, EFT can help reestablish healthy boundaries.)

What delights you? Where are your edges? What are your boundaries? Again, getting your needs or desires met begins with identifying what they are. Communicating them to your partner comes after that.

Did you ever play the game Marco Polo as a kid? A blindfolded player who is "it" shouts "Marco!" and sighted players shout "Polo!" This call and response takes place repeatedly until the blindfolded player acoustically locates a sighted player.

Relationships are like Marco Polo. You spend a lot of time stumbling around in the dark trying to connect. When you're feeling disoriented, lost, and lonely, there's nothing more gratifying than having your questioning "Marco?" met with your beloved's resounding "Polo!" and then finding your way to each other.

CHAPTER 3
TAKING MATTERS INTO YOUR OWN HANDS

The expression "Know thyself" has been attributed to many. No one implies that it's easy, but it's worth striving for. Self-knowledge enables us to live in a way that's consistent with our values. It helps us make good decisions, be fully present in relationships, advocate for ourselves, and ask for what we need. We all have a voice, but it's through self-knowledge that we learn what to say.

Sexually speaking, self-knowledge has had an interesting history. In the mid- to late 1800s, doctors diagnosed women whose emotions were "excessive and unmanageable" as having "hysteria," which, like "hysterectomy," comes from Greek word for uterus. Physicians thought the condition originated in that organ and cured it via "medicinal massage" of the genitals, resulting in a "paroxysm."

In other words, doctors believed that the cure for hysteria was a medically facilitated orgasm. (Maines, 1999) It's hard to believe now, but at the time, no one thought women *had* orgasms—only men were thought to be capable of that, physiologically.

Not surprisingly, the treatment for hysteria became so popular among patients that the doctors who administered it developed repetitive strain injuries. Dr. Joseph Mortimer Granville solved the problem by inventing an electric massager that reduced the duration of treatment to a fraction of the time, caused a paroxysm almost every time, and also helped alleviate doctors' pain. (Stern, 2012)

By 1904, these massagers were advertised in women's magazines and sold openly in the Sears and Roebuck catalog, eliminating the need for doctors to perform the treatment. However, thanks to early pornographic films, in which these massagers were depicted, men finally made the connection between paroxysms and sex.

Vibrators disappeared from the scene in the 1920s. Though they resurfaced during the sexual revolution of the sixties and seventies, they didn't really come out of the closet again until the late 1990s, thanks, in part, to the television series *Sex and the City* (Vineyard, 2012). They still haven't been universally accepted, though. As of this writing, it's still illegal to sell a vibrator in Alabama. (Schwartz, 2014)

While women were being brought to orgasm by physicians who believed the treatment restored them to health, men were being told that masturbation was a form of "self-abuse" that could cause blindness, acne, tuberculosis, memory loss, and epilepsy, among other grave conditions. (Kellogg, 1881)

If you're feeling at all conflicted about "knowing thyself" through self-pleasuring, it's no wonder! We're bombarded by images of idealized relationships and two-dimensional depictions of sexuality that embrace and promote a very narrow definition of sex. When Dr. Rachel Maines, author of *The Technology of Orgasm,* was asked how it was possible that Victorian doctors didn't *know* they were masturbating patients to orgasm, she said "Well, we all know–with a capital K–that real sex is penetration to male orgasm. When there isn't penetration to orgasm, they figured, there isn't sex." (Kling)

But sexual pleasure doesn't require the presence of another, and it doesn't require penetration. By the age of 20, more than 95 percent of men and 60 percent of women have self-pleasured to orgasm, though some studies suggest a larger gap between men and women (Kinsey Institute).

In a *Psychology Today* article titled "The Masturbation Gap," Noam Shpancer, Ph. D., says that difference matters. "The discrepancy with regard to masturbation is doubly problematic because masturbation, it turns out, is a particularly important predictor of sexual health and happiness for women, more so than for men," he says. "One of the best predictors of whether a woman will be able to achieve orgasm in her sexual relations is a history of masturbation in adolescence." (Shpancer, 2010)

Artist Sophia Wallace has started what she calls the "Cliteracy Project" to educate people about an organ that wasn't fully mapped internally and externally until 1998. It has twice as many nerve endings as the penis and is the only organ in the human body whose sole function is to provide pleasure. But in a recent study, nearly 30 percent of female college students couldn't locate the clitoris on a diagram of the vulva. (Kolodny & Genuske, 2015) Women need to make it their business to know their own bodies. Pleasure is just one of the reasons.

My client Greta came to see me because she wanted to have an orgasm. I ask her if she knew much about her body, such as how it works sexually, and she immediately turned purple. We jumped right in and used EFT to diminish the embarrassment she felt. When the emotional intensity decreased, Greta said she'd been raised in a household where people didn't talk about such things. Now married, she sensed that there was more to sex than pleasing her husband. She teared up as she described herself as frigid, and she felt ashamed about her lack of feeling. She knew that her husband really wanted her to feel pleasure. We used EFT on her feelings of shame. Greta's homework assignment was to spend some time in the shower touching and sensing her entire body and using EFT on any negative emotions that came up in the process.

The following week, Greta reported feeling better about speaking openly to me about her situation and, through her homework, had learned that her body did feel strong sensations. I asked her to remember any times in her past where she felt ashamed of her body, and several memories came up around middle school. She had developed much sooner than her classmates, and we used EFT on several memories of classmates making fun of her. She also remembered her parents' insistence that any physical contact with boys was "a sin." And she remembered a high school classmate's comment about self-pleasuring: "That is the most revolting thing I can imagine! It's not real if you aren't with a guy." We used EFT on all those memories until the emotional intensity that Greta felt around them was gone.

Greta's homework the following week was to explore her genitals and learn what types of touch and pressure felt best where. Again, she was to use EFT on any feelings of fear or resistance that arose while doing so, or while reflecting on the experience.

Later that week, Greta called me to report that she'd not only done her homework, she'd had an orgasm! During our next session, we worked through her feelings of embarrassment about sharing this new information about herself with her husband. By our last session, Greta had reached her goal of having an orgasm, achieved a new level of intimacy and communication with her husband, and felt empowered by the fact that she could literally take responsibility for her own pleasure with her hands, both through EFT and self-pleasuring.

I recommend that my clients take the time to explore themselves and "map" what feels pleasurable and where. If that idea repulses you for any reason, use EFT on any painful emotions and memories that arise until the thought of self-pleasuring no longer evokes a negative reaction in you. You'll learn how to do EFT later in this book. After you've read all the way through to Chapter 8, circle back here and map your body's pleasure zones.

Ten reasons to self-pleasure and two reasons not to

WHEN SELF-PLEASURING CAN MAKE THINGS BETTER

Here are some ways in which self-pleasuring can help you know yourself, heal, and experience a more fulfilling sex life.

1. Self-discovery

If you're in your reproductive years, self-pleasuring can help you understand how your body changes during your menstrual cycle. When are you more likely to feel aroused? How does what feels good to you change over the course of your cycle? Are your breasts tender sometimes, for example? Is your libido higher when you ovulate? Do orgasms relieve cramps?

Self-pleasuring helps you be present to your body and fosters awareness and knowledge. Communicating that knowledge can help improve sex with your partner.

2. Getting to know your post-childbirth body

I also recommend self-pleasuring to women after childbirth, to give them an opportunity to explore and feel comfortable with their changed bodies. Your body is never the same after carrying and giving birth to a child, and you may fear that sex with your partner will cause pain afterward. If you're breastfeeding, you may also be concerned about leaking milk during sex. Or, you may feel unattractive and undesirable in your post-baby body.

Those fears are great ones to use EFT on, and it's usually better to give them an opportunity to arise through self-pleasuring (so you can clear them using EFT), than it is to have them arise when you resume having sex with your partner.

3. Healing after surgery

If you've had surgery (such as a hysterectomy or mastectomy) self-pleasuring can help you address any changes that negatively impact your self-perception, or that affect the way you and your partner interact sexually.

As you self-pleasure, painful beliefs or fears may arise. Notice them, and know that you can use EFT to work on them later. Clearing them before you resume making love with your partner will increase enjoyment for both of you.

4. Healing from sexual abuse

As you recover from sexual abuse, self-pleasuring can be a wonderful step in your healing journey. When you're alone, the presence of another poses no threat, and you have plenty of time to take self-exploration step-by-step. If uncomfortable memories come up, use EFT.

5. Getting out of a rut

If it seems like you and your partner go through the same routine every time you're intimate, I recommend self-pleasuring to help you remember what feels good to you, what parts of your body feel the most pleasure, and what types of stimulation you like.

Once you've identified what feels good, tap on any fears you have about telling your partner what you need. The more you know about yourself, and are able to communicate to your partner, the more you empower your partner to pleasure you.

6. If it's been a while since you've had sex

I also recommend self-pleasuring for those who haven't had a partner for a while. If you're feeling afraid of being with another person sexually, it's good to get reacquainted with your own body and tap on any fears that arise about becoming intimate with someone again.

Are you afraid your partner might find your naked body unattractive? Are you afraid of getting hurt again? Use EFT on anything that's creating a barrier between yourself and the intimacy you long for.

7. Turning up your libido

The more orgasms you have, the more you'll want, and self-pleasuring can help crank up your desire. If you used to be "hot and ready to go" most of the time, but things have slowed down or ground to a halt, you may simply have low libido. To help get your libido back, start self-pleasuring.

8. Accommodating different sexual appetites

If your desire for sex is greater than that of your partner, self-pleasuring is a way to even things out and take responsibility for your own sexual fulfillment without resenting or casting blame on someone else.

9. Paving the way for a sexual partner

If you don't have a sexual partner, but want one, self-pleasuring is a good way to explore any resistance you might have to manifesting one in your life.

Are you blocking the manifestation of a sexual partner? If so, what else are you resisting? Are you capable of receiving pleasure in other areas of your life? If not, loving yourself paves the way for receiving the love of others.

If you have a block around self-acceptance, self-pleasuring could bring it to the surface, which will give you an opportunity to eliminate it through EFT.

10. When intercourse is out of the question

Self-pleasuring doesn't have to be solitary. If you or your partner are ill, are separated for an extended period of time, or have a sexually transmitted disease, you can still enjoy each other's company (in person, on the phone, or via video conference) by self-pleasuring together or by pleasuring each other.

WHEN SELF-PLEASURING CAN MAKE THINGS WORSE

There are a few circumstances in which self-pleasuring can be detrimental to you or your partner.

1. When there's only one road to Rome

If self-pleasuring is the *only* way you can reach orgasm, even in a relationship, I recommend you stop and give your nervous system a chance to rewire. This is especially true if for people who have come to rely on porn to reach orgasm. It can take months of no porn, and no self-pleasuring, to reboot your brain. (Your Brain on Porn, 2010)

2. When self-pleasuring is an avoidance technique

If you find yourself having sex less often with your partner and self-pleasuring more, it's time to stop self-pleasuring and repair your relationship. This is a chicken-and-egg problem. Does a lack of sexual intimacy cause a couple to drift apart, or does the fact that a couple drifted apart cause less sexual intimacy?

CHAPTER 4
WHAT EFT IS AND HOW IT WORKS

Whenever I meet someone, and we go through the ritual of telling each other our names and professions, my new acquaintance inevitably asks "What's EFT?" And, whether I'm on a plane, at a party, or attending one of my kids' school events, that question is usually followed by "How does EFT work?"

"What is EFT?" is pretty easy to answer: it's a combination of acupuncture point stimulation and focused thought. When you "do EFT," you tap on your own acupoints while describing how you feel about a specific problem or memory. This often relieves both physical and emotional symptoms.

"How does EFT work?" is a far harder question to answer. Sometimes, scientists start with things that don't work and "fix" them. The smallpox vaccine, for example, "fixed" the problem of smallpox, a disease that killed as many as 300,000,000 people in the 20th century alone and was declared eradicated in 1980.

Sometimes, despite all their efforts, scientists can't figure out how things *do* work–for example, gravity (Mosher, 2007). EFT is a little of both. Its roots are in Chinese medicine, which was created more than 3,000 years ago to "fix" all kinds of health-related problems. But, like gravity, scientists can't fully explain *why* it works, yet. If you need to understand why something works before you try it, EFT may not be for you. But gravity is keeping you on the planet every day, whether scientists fully understand it or not. So why not give EFT a try?

As I write, 60 peer-reviewed reports or studies on EFT have been published in scientific journals, and the overwhelming majority demonstrated a positive outcome. The conditions involved in these studies included depression, physical pain, tension headaches, fibromyalgia syndrome, post-traumatic stress disorder (PTSD), food cravings and weight loss, phobias, test anxiety, and public speaking anxiety. You'll find a link to one of the most comprehensive collections of EFT research available at tapyourpower.net/book, including many of the studies I just referenced.

Let's break EFT down into its components and explore each one individually. EFT entails:

- A specific event or condition that you're working on

- The emotion(s) you feel in response to that event or condition

- The origin, location, or source of that emotion in your body

- Self-acceptance

1. Tapping acupoints

A specific event or condition

Trying to tap on "all the times" or "every time" something happened in your life can overwhelm you, make EFT less effective, and actually increase your stress response. Breaking experiences into segments makes them more manageable. When you bring a *specific* incident to mind, it activates the frontal lobes of the brain and makes a thought or memory more accessible to change (Ecker, Ticic, & Hulley, 2012).

Memories come in two types: conscious and unconscious. You can recall conscious memories in detail, for example: "The time I drove down I-75 with my family on the way to the Everglades, and we ate bologna sandwiches in the back of the station wagon."

Unconscious memories, on the other hand, are often associated with early childhood experiences or traumatic events. Your conscious mind can repress or forget them to protect you, but your body remembers, which is why you sometimes have a physical stress response without knowing why. For example, say your palms sweat and your heart beats more rapidly at the very thought of putting on a bathing suit, but you have no idea why. That physical response may have its origins in an early experience you've forgotten, like the humiliation of having your bathing suit come off after jumping into a pool.

Using EFT on such an incident may be achieving what psychologists call counter-conditioning. The original conditioned response of embarrassment includes the uncomfortable emotional and physical reactions that come up when you think about putting on a bathing suit. EFT may be creating a re-conditioned response, enabling you to remember the event without embarrassment. In other words, tapping may "rewire" the brain to respond differently to the same thoughts or memories.

I've often seen clients laugh at memories that, only moments before, they'd found so upsetting they had trouble talking about them. Counter-conditioning offers the brain another, more empowering way to respond.

Until the 1990s, scientists didn't think memories could be changed, especially if they were formed at a time when people experienced strong emotions. But research has shown that habits and patterns resulting from such memories can be changed or eradicated when certain conditions are met (Decker & Feinstein, 2015).

2. The emotion(s) you feel in response to that event or condition

EFT may also be effective because you have to put your feelings into words when you do it. A study conducted by researchers at UCLA shows that expressing negative emotions helps diffuse them. Researchers split arachnophobes (people who are afraid of spiders) into four groups, and then exposed them to a live tarantula in an open container.

Then, they asked members of:

- The first group to describe what they were feeling in great detail.

- The second group to make statements such as, "That little spider can't hurt me; I'm not afraid of it."

- The third group to say something completely irrelevant.

- The fourth group to say nothing at all.

A week later, when they were re-exposed to the tarantula, members of the first group got closer to the spider and experienced a lower stress response than members of the other three groups. In fact, researchers found that the subjects who used more emotionally-fueled language in describing their fear stood a greater chance of overcoming it. (Kircanski, Lieberman, & Craske, 2012)

3. The origin, location, or source of that emotion in the body

Part of the EFT formula entails locating emotions in our bodies. Some people find this easy to do, while others find it very difficult or nearly impossible. Ongoing clinical evidence, especially in the field of trauma resolution, shows that finding the connection between our emotions and our physical bodies makes healing from traumatic events more achievable. (For an excellent book on this topic, I recommend Bessel van der Kolk's *The Body Keeps the Score: Brain, Mind, and Body in the Healing of Trauma*.)

4. Self-acceptance

Self-acceptance, in the form of a true self-affirming statement made while tapping, is an important aspect of EFT. It may not be possible to measure the importance of self-acceptance, but clinical psychologist David Feinstein suggests that tapping while you make statements of self-acceptance may "facilitate a somatic [bodily] implanting of the affirmation." (Feinstein, 2015)

Don't confuse self-acceptance with self-esteem. Albert Ellis, the American psychologist who authored the book *The Myth of Self-Esteem,* said "Self-esteem is the greatest sickness known to man or woman because it's conditional." (Epstein, 2001) Ellis advocated unconditional self-acceptance (USA) in which "the individual fully and unconditionally accepts himself whether or not he behaves intelligently, correctly, or competently and whether or not other people approve, respect, or love him." (Ellis & Grieger, 1977)

Accepting what you've experienced, said, and felt opens a powerful window into healing, and making statements of self-acceptance while you send electromagnetic signals into your brain via tapping may prove to be a potent element of EFT.

5. Tapping acupoints

Tapping the acupoints involved in EFT sends sensory information to the brain. Mechanically stimulating the bony areas beneath those acupoints also creates what's called a piezoelectric effect, which converts tapping pressure to electromagnetic energy that may increase the flow of information to key areas of the brain.

Researchers have used electroencephalograms (EEGs) to observe subjects' brains before and after tapping. By measuring brainwaves, they discovered that tapping can change electrical activity in the brain. In one study, subjects recalled a traumatic memory, at which time their brainwaves were chaotic. After they tapped, their brainwaves normalized (Swingle, Pulos, & Swingle, 2005). Another EEG study, in which subjects tapped after they experienced traumatic car accidents, demonstrated that tapping decreased arousal in the right frontal cortex. (Diepold & Goldstein, 2008)

Researchers (Hui, et al., 2000) from the Harvard University Medical School found that when specific acupoints were activated, there was an observable calming effect on the amygdala, which is a critical part of the brain's emotional center. Some use the metaphor of a smoke alarm to refer to the amygdala–which is kind of close. Like a smoke alarm, your amygdala constantly monitors your environment for danger. But unlike a smoke alarm, it also triggers the cascade of hormones and physiological responses that empower you to fight or flee.

Stress and trauma can cause the amygdala to get "stuck on," and when that happens, the overabundance of adrenaline and cortisol in your system can be detrimental to your health. That's why research published in the *Journal of Nervous and Mental Disease* (Church, Yount, & Brooks, 2012) is heartening. Researchers found that a single 50-minute EFT session resulted in a 24 percent reduction in salivary cortisol levels. Tapping appears to recalibrate our alarm system, disarm hyper-arousal, and reduce stress hormones, so the body can respond to real threats more appropriately. By reducing stress, tapping helps us get out of "survival mode" and frees us to be more present, solve problems more creatively, and engage with others more whole-heartedly.

The ability of the brain to change how thoughts, memories, sensations, and patterns of behavior are processed is called "neuroplasticity," and the fact that EFT seems to facilitate neuroplastic re-wiring may be why it's such a powerful tool for change.

CHAPTER 5
BEFORE YOU BEGIN—
PAVING THE WAY
FOR HEALING

I know you're reading this book to help yourself heal, and because I'm invested in making that possible for you, I don't want you to dive right into doing EFT just yet. There are a few things to take care of first that will greatly increase the likelihood that EFT will be effective for you.

Before you start using EFT on specific issues that you want to heal, let's take a look at some potential obstacles that could sabotage your efforts. If your brain were an iceberg, only the very tip of it, your conscious mind, would be above the water, and the vast majority of it, your subconscious mind, would be underwater. It wasn't the visible part of an iceberg that sunk the Titanic, so it behooves us to respect what lies beneath the surface.

Addressing fears that may prevent you from healing

Let's start with fears. Generally speaking, humans aren't fond of change—even positive changes like healing. It's natural to be a bit fearful of the unknown, but your fears may throw a roadblock into the path of healing.

Are any of the following true for you?

- I'm scared of uncovering an issue that's too big, frightening, or dark for me to handle.

- I'm afraid that my partner might feel hurt or offended to discover that I'm dissatisfied with our sex life.

- I'm scared of causing a rift in our relationship.

- My current relationship might have to change if I change.

- What if I discover that my current partner is the wrong one for me?

- What if I suddenly want more sex?

- I'm afraid of having to actually talk about sex with my partner.

- My partner might judge or reject me when I express my desires.

- I'm embarrassed about my sexual preferences or what others will think, feel, or say about them.

- I'm scared that I might not get what I want, so I'd rather not ask than be disappointed or rejected.

Carefully consider the fears, both listed and unlisted, that are true for you, and tap on each one (by following the instructions in Chapter 8) while listening to your inner voice. Following your intuition may lead you to other fears, and the further you go, the more specific you can get.

Specificity super-charges tapping. EFT is like WD-40®. The little red tube that comes with every can enables you to apply it with pinpoint accuracy to get things unstuck and moving again. EFT requires the same type of precision. For example, say you find that the statement above that most resonates for you is "I'm afraid that my partner might feel hurt or offended to discover that I'm dissatisfied with our sex life." You could tap on that, but it would work a lot better if you wrote down specific times in your current relationship, or in any other relationship, when someone was hurt or offended by something you said, and then tapped on each individual memory.

Outsmarting your subconscious mind

You may have trouble healing until you confront the possibility that your conscious and subconscious minds might not be on the same page. Although your conscious mind may fully embrace the notion of healing, your subconscious mind may be invested in preventing it. Why? Because there may be hidden benefits to your situation.

"Wait," you say. "Are you implying that I may be deliberately holding on to the very thing I want to heal because it benefits me somehow? You're out of your mind!"

I don't blame you. That's what I thought, too. In EFT, hidden benefits are called "secondary gains," and when I first read about secondary gains, I was downright angry! I'd been battling an autoimmune condition for 12 years and had searched everywhere for a solution, yet the EFT information stated clearly that if I'd tried everything (which I had) and nothing had worked (which it hadn't), I needed to consider the possibility that my illness offered a benefit that I wasn't willing to let go of. I was struggling with multiple symptoms, including weight gain and the inability to lose weight, fatigue, headaches, dry skin, hair loss, and achiness. "How could they even suggest that I *wanted* my illness!" I thought.

But over the years, I've come to recognize that feeling righteous indignation is a sign that I need to pay attention. As I honestly explored my situation, I realized that there were three benefits to my illness after all. 1) My symptoms began after I had a stillborn child, and the anger I felt toward God was empowering. 2) It was easier to blame my weight gain on an illness than on my eating habits. 3) I'd developed quite an expertise around alternative remedies for my condition, and I rather enjoyed being an expert. These were the "benefits" that prevented me from healing.

Taking the time to uncover hidden benefits makes it more likely that EFT will be effective for you. Here are some areas you can explore:

Safety: What is your condition protecting you from? A classic hidden benefit is one that often underlies being overweight. Subconsciously holding on to extra weight can be a way to protect yourself from unwanted sexual attention.

Worthiness: If you don't think you deserve to heal, it's going to be hard to get better. Do you feel worthy of healing?

Fear of change: What do you risk losing if you heal?

Identity: Have you identified yourself with this problem? Who would you be without it?

Here's an example from my practice in which safety, worthiness, and identity issues arose. Leanna avoided having sex for six months after giving birth. When I asked her why, she said she was afraid it would hurt. We tapped on her fear that intercourse would hurt, and then she said, "I don't want to get over my fear of it hurting, because if I do, my husband will see my body, and pregnancy and childbirth have changed my body so much that I'm afraid he'll reject me." (Refusing sex kept her safe from rejection.)

We tapped on that fear, which dissolved. When I asked her to imagine being naked in front of her husband, she said that she couldn't imagine having sex one moment and breastfeeding her baby the next. She found it difficult to reconcile her roles as a lover and a mother. (Identifying solely with her role as a mother caused her to reject her identity as a lover.)

We tapped on that fear, and again it collapsed. A week later, I asked Leanna to think about having sex with her husband,

and she said she didn't deserve pleasure, because she hadn't been a good mother. She'd recently used a "cry-it-out" method to get her baby to sleep through the night and was feeling terribly guilty about it. (She didn't consider herself worthy of sexual intimacy.)

We tapped on the guilt she felt. Within a few days, she reported feeling sexual desire again and was enjoying sex with her husband. She laughed and said that she couldn't believe all the thoughts and feelings she wasn't aware of that had been contributing to her problem.

Nowhere is Walt Whitman's encouragement to "be curious, not judgmental" more relevant than in the process of finding hidden benefits. When I bring this subject up with my clients, I do so gently and compassionately. "I know you want to heal," I say. "But if there's a small part of you that isn't on board with your healing, let's have a discussion with it."

Secondary gains usually lie under the surface of our conscious awareness. It's important to know this, especially if you're thinking that this section of the book doesn't apply to you, because you're 100 percent certain that you want to heal. Even if you are, isn't it worth taking the time to make sure that EFT works as effectively as it can by asking yourself a few questions?

If you discover a hidden benefit, there's no need to beat yourself up over it. Discovering and addressing it is actually a huge win because it means you've outsmarted your subconscious mind and removed obstacles to healing!

Here are some questions to ask yourself:

- Is there a way in which my current condition/circumstance benefits me?

- What would I have to give up if I healed?

- Is there any aspect of my condition/circumstance that actually feels safe or comforting?

- How would others around me have to change if I healed?

- Do I define myself by my condition/circumstance?

- Who would I be if this condition/circumstance wasn't a major part of my life story?

- Does anger/outrage/a sense of injustice make me feel empowered? Who would I be if I let that go?

- Do I identify myself with or have I found camaraderie among others who have experienced my condition/circumstance?

- Do I consider myself a survivor of my condition/circumstance? Is being a survivor an important part of my identity?

- Does identifying myself as a victim of this condition/circumstance help me gain attention or sympathy that I'd find hard to give up?

If you discover hidden benefits, print out the journal template at tapyourpower.net/book, and then tap on each benefit by following the instructions in Chapter 8. If none of these questions seem to hit the nail on the head, use the following as a setup statement when tapping (this will make more sense after you've read Chapter 8): "Even though I don't know why some part of me wants to hold on to this problem, I deeply and completely accept myself." This setup statement may jog your subconscious mind into showing you what the inner conflict is. If it does, tap on that, too.

If you can't find hidden benefits on your own, but you've been struggling with your condition for more than six months, you may need the help of a seasoned EFT practitioner to help you find them.

When to work with an EFT practitioner

The EFT process is like a scavenger hunt, with one discovery leading to the next. The goal of the hunt is healing, but sometimes, painful things that your subconscious mind has kept buried may pop up to the surface. Or, you may recall memories that your body has been protecting you from through the miracle of dissociation.

Dissociation is like a psychological "eject" button that enables us to avoid pain, violation, or trauma while it's taking place. The downside of dissociation is that, after traumatic experiences, we may not feel safe enough in our own bodies to "come home" again. Intimacy can be challenging for those who don't feel safe in their bodies.

Another way our bodies protect us is through the fight-or-flight response. When we perceive a threat, our bodies flood us with the adrenaline, cortisol, and glucose we need to fight off or flee from danger. The downside of the fight-or-flight response is that thoughts and memories can trigger it—even when no physical threat is present—and it's hard to think clearly when you're in survival mode.

As the saying goes, "the way beyond is through." So here you are, stuck between wanting to heal and knowing that you may have to go through some uncomfortable terrain to get there. What to do? Know that if your healing journey gets uncomfortable, you don't have to go it alone. In fact, in some cases, it's best not to. It's best to ask for help if you:

- Have experienced or witnessed a terrifying event and are having symptoms such as uncontrollable thoughts, severe anxiety, nightmares, or flashbacks.

- Have been exposed to social or interpersonal trauma over a long period of time and felt disempowered or trapped, with no viable escape route.

- Suspect childhood sexual abuse or know that you were sexually abused.

Although people who have experienced trauma of a non-sexual nature may encounter one or more of the situations listed below, those who have experienced sexual trauma (whether they recall it or not) do so more frequently. (Committee on Health Care for Underserved Women, 2011)

If you're experiencing any of the following, do not use EFT on your own. Consider working with a professional EFT coach or with a licensed health care professional who is qualified to work with your particular issue.

- Addictions, ranging from smoking to alcohol to drugs.

- Eating disorders or obesity

- Depression or anxiety

- Nightmares or flashbacks

- Chronic pain, especially in the pelvis

- A low pain threshold

- Fifty or more intercourse partners

- A sexually transmitted infection

- A pregnancy in early adolescence

- Find yourself repeatedly exploited by untrustworthy people

- Strong sensations of anxiety that show up in your throat, such as gaggling or choking

- Wearing baggy clothes to hide your body or being afraid to remove your clothes in front of your partner, a doctor, or at the gym

- Self-mutilation or cutting

- Trouble expressing anger at others

- Trouble being near others who are angry

- Finding anger erotic

- Obsession with suicidal thoughts

- Compulsive cleanliness

- Compulsive checking of door locks

- "Illogical" fears about particular places or people

- Strong fear of, or resistance to, having sex

- Engaging in sexually risky behavior on a regular basis

- The inability to remember events from childhood

- The inability to remember events from childhood is the symptom that many find most disconcerting, so let's talk about why it happens and what it means.

Our brains protect us by keeping some memories conscious and others unconscious. We couldn't function if we remembered everything all the time. The inability to remember is also a normal part of childhood. Because the brain isn't fully developed, episodic memories before age four are almost impossible to access consciously. This is called childhood amnesia, and everyone experiences it.

Being unable to remember events from early childhood doesn't mean you were sexually abused, but if you're also experiencing some of the other things on the preceding list, you may have been. Your body will remember what your brain cannot. Sexually charged memories often come up as fragments or snippets of information. Clients sometimes come to me with only a memory of themselves scared in bed, or hiding in a closet, or with the thought of a seemingly innocuous item, such as a teddy bear.

What these snippets have in common is that they disturb or provoke anxiety in the client. Often, my clients feel a sense of safety that gives them access to things they never remembered before. I once worked with a young man who was beaten for playing doctor with a young girl when he was a child. What he remembered was taking his pants off in an attic when he was about five years old. He was terrified of what he'd find if he allowed himself to remember more. At the same time, he felt terrified of continuing his life without knowing. After we tapped, he was able to recall the complete memory. He actually did take his pants off, and the little girl took her dress off. They lay there next to each other, and then she said, "We are making a baby." That's it.

As they were about to put their clothes back on, his mother came in and saw them. Later, when his father came home from work, he was beaten. My client's brain had prevented him from accessing the entire memory, even the innocent parts, because of the beating that followed.

I've come to realize that sometimes fear is just fear. As was the case with my client, we sometimes don't remember an event because of its aftermath, not because of the actual event.

CHAPTER 6
A FEW OF YOUR FAVORITE THINGS

In *The Sound of Music*, Maria, the governess to the seven von Trapp children, sings a song about the things that make her feel better when she's sad. They include things like:

- Raindrops on roses

- Whiskers on kittens

- Bright copper kettles

- Warm woolen mittens

Her complete list includes other things that delight her, such as sounds that fill her with eager anticipation and sights like packages that make her wonder what's inside. You know how the song goes. You probably won't be able to get it out of your head for the rest of the day!

Maria is singing about resources: the things that raise her spirits when she feels bad. But crisp apple strudels and schnitzel with noodles probably aren't among *your* favorite things, and it's important to come up with a list of your own. What makes *you* feel better when you're feeling unsettled, tense, or hypervigilant? What brings relief when you're feeling disconnected from your body—when you're so busy ruminating about the past and worrying about the future that you're unable to be *present*? What makes you feel safe, grounded, and happy?

Resources bring you to a state of integration and wholeness. They give you a sense of wellbeing and bring you to your highest expression of yourself. Things like consuming too much alcohol, using drugs, or binge eating might make you feel better in the short term, but in the long run, they don't count as resources. As you've probably found, they *compound* your problems instead of helping you overcome them.

Identifying your resources before you need them gives you a way to reestablish balance. When you have a bad day, you'll know exactly what to do to feel better. Before you continue to the next chapter, please write a list of the activities that nourish and ground you, and put it on the fridge or on your phone. When you *use* this list, you're "resourcing."

Outer resources

Anything that helps connect you to the planet and to your body will help you enjoy greater sexual intimacy. The more you develop your senses, the more you'll be able to enjoy them. When sommeliers evaluate a wine, for example, they engage their sense of vision, smell, and taste. They evaluate the color and body of a wine, discern its aroma, and finally, they taste it. Experienced sommeliers can tell what kind of grape the wine is made of, what type of barrel it was aged in, the region it's from, what vineyard it was grown in, and the year it was bottled. In the process of learning to taste wine, sommeliers learn to be discerning, learn how to pair wines with food, and above all, *they learn what they like.*

If you don't know what you like, try out new things and figure out what truly nourishes you. If you do know what rebalances you, create a list and *use it.* And if you feel any resistance to resourcing, tap. For example, if you're a stay-at-home mom who feels guilty about carving out time for yourself, tap on it. If you're a career woman who doesn't think downtime is productive, tap on it. And if you think pleasure feels self-indulgent and sinful, tap on it. You'll find tapping instructions in Chapter 8.

Here's a list of ideas to get you started on outer resources. Everyone's list is unique, so pick any of the resources below that appeal to you and add new ones of your own.

- Gardening

- Singing, playing, or listening to music

- Yoga

- Walking, dancing, or exercising in a way that you find pleasurable

- Being in nature or looking at pictures of nature if you can't be in it

- Spending time with your pet

- Cooking

- Reading

- Knitting, sewing, or other handwork

- Drawing, doodling, or coloring a mandala

- Enjoying the performing or visual arts

- Writing

- Meditating

- Having a conversation with a friend

- Getting a massage or foot rub

- Walking barefoot on the beach or in the grass

- Smelling essential oils

- Watching a comedy

- Yawning and stretching

- Drinking a cup of coffee, tea, or hot chocolate

- Taking a bubble bath

- Repeating a mantra

- Making love

- Self-pleasuring

Inner resources

Unlike outer resources, you can access inner resources anywhere and don't need equipment, skills, or a specific location. Inner resources include:

- **Recalling a memory of someone with whom you always felt safe.** The more senses you can incorporate into your memory, the better. For example, when I recall being with my grandmother, I immediately feel peaceful. I can remember the sound of her voice, the feeling of breaking eggs into a mixing bowl, and the smell of cookies baking.

- **Recalling or imagining a safe place.** My imaginary safe place is a meadow with a brook babbling through it and mist rising from the water. The meadow is surrounded by forest, and sunlight filters through the tree branches, casting dappled light on the forest floor. Everything is lush and green, and the temperature of the air is just right. Again, the more senses you can involve when recalling or imagining a safe place, the better. If you'd like to try a guided visualization, which will help you do just that, Belleruth Naperstek's recordings are a great place to start. You'll find recordings on all sorts of topics at healthjourneys.com.

- **Connecting with spiritual guides.** Is there a spiritual guide who makes you feel accompanied on life's journey? A being who makes you feel safe and unconditionally loved? It could be Jesus, the Buddha, deities, saints, fairies, angels, totem animals, or the spirit of a departed loved one. This is where I call on the spirit of my deceased daughter, Hannah. Losing her was the most painful experience I ever had. But now, when I sense her presence, I feel comfort, love, and know that everything's going to be OK.

Why are we talking about resourcing? Because sometimes, in the process of tapping, you can recall memories or events that you'd forgotten about—and they can occasionally surprise or upset you. If that happens, you know what to do. Together with Orienting EFT, which you'll learn about in Chapter 9, you'll have a list of inner and outer resources, as well as a skill, that make up a toolbox that you can draw from.

But you don't have to wait until you feel bad to resource. In fact, the more you do it, the more resilient you'll be when trouble does arise. I call this "preventative resourcing." Take a look at your list and figure out which things you could do every day. Which things could you do weekly, once a month, and annually?

Now, put them all on your calendar, and *do* them!

CHAPTER 7
WAIT. HOW DID I GET HERE?

My daughter *hates* blueberries. She doesn't know where that aversion originated, but I do. When she was three, she caught a stomach virus around the time I made my first homemade blueberry ice cream. After she ate it, she threw up, and there was purple everywhere: on the carpets, the sheets, her clothes. Everywhere. My daughter was scared and in pain, and it doesn't surprise me one bit that she made a subconscious connection between blueberries and nausea. In her three-year-old mind, blueberries *caused* her to get sick, and she never wanted to experience that again.

I pick my battles with my kids. Blueberries aren't hard to avoid, and my daughter can lead a happy and fulfilling life without them, so I just let it go. But if she had an aversion to something that truly limited her, I'd say, "Let's work on that."

Driving is an example. I had a client who couldn't drive for ten years after she had a car accident, and her fear of driving limited where she could work, where she shopped, where she obtained services, and with whom she spent time. After we tapped, I called her several times to see how she was doing. When I couldn't reach her, I left voicemail and started to worry. Finally, she called back and said, "I've been too busy driving everywhere to call you!" One EFT session, and she was back in the saddle.

In my daughter's case, her hatred of blueberries was a mystery to her, but not to me. In my client's case, the cause of her inability to drive was obvious to both of us. But in *most* cases, neither my clients nor I know what the *real* cause of their issue is, because the presenting issue is almost never the source of the problem. It's usually just the tip of an iceberg.

For example, one of my clients was having trouble starting a specialty wedding dress business. Francine was a savvy marketer, having worked in the sales and marketing departments of a number of bridal gown and evening wear manufacturers. On her intake form, she mentioned that when she thought of writing sales copy for her website, all she did was procrastinate.

Procrastination usually stems from a globalized fear, so I asked Francine to close her eyes and imagine herself writing a tag line and some copy for her website, assuring her that she'd have all the time in the world to refine it later. Francine came up with a few statements that included words like "feel good," "you're unique," and "you'll receive one-on-one attention." When I asked her to read them aloud, she became agitated.

We tapped over and over again, in silence, to lower the intensity of the emotions she was feeling, and then Francine was able to tell me why those particular statements were triggering for her. She'd been molested at age 10, and her abuser had seduced her with statements such as, "You're special" and "I'll make you feel good." Gently working through these issues with EFT ended Francine's problem with procrastination, removed the creative blocks that prevented her from promoting her business, and helped address the root cause of these problems—the sexual abuse she'd experienced as a child. But we had *no idea* where we'd end up when we started tapping.

Identifying "tappable" issues

There are two big clues that can help you identify "tappable" issues:

- A response that's completely out of proportion to a person or situation.

- An issue that prevents you from achieving your goals.

LITTLE STIMULUS, BIG RESPONSE

My spiritual mentor says that, when he's having a meal with his wife and her chewing annoys him, it's time to step away and think about what's really bothering him. Wise man.

My former husband and I used to share an office, and the fact that I didn't put the stapler back in its cubby drove him nuts. In retrospect, I'm sure I was at least a little passive-aggressive in leaving that stapler out as a way of saying,

"I'm an adult now, and by God no one's going to tell me to clean up anymore." When I was a child, my mother told me incessantly to clean my room, but for some reason, it was in my marriage that I decided to take a stand.

When something insignificant like a stapler starts a war, you can be almost certain that it's not about the stapler. But it gives you a place to start tapping, and you can see where that leads.

LIMITING ISSUES

When something keeps preventing you from achieving your goals, and success seems perpetually out of reach, you've probably stumbled onto a tappable issue.

One of my clients had several master's degrees, but found herself perpetually jobless. Although she was able to get jobs, her employers usually let her go after six months to a year. The reasons they gave included her inability to get to work on time and her inability to meet deadlines. Esther had done years of personal-growth work and was aware that this was likely some form of self-sabotage. Yet she couldn't prevent the pattern from repeating.

I asked Esther why she lost her last job, and she said she'd been put in charge of a project in a large nonprofit that included communication with several high-profile donors. She was thrilled that she'd landed her dream job and felt completely comfortable with her tasks. She brought in others to form her support team and everything seemed to go well–until a new manager took over her department. She noted that he was a man with an "aggressive" personality around whom she felt nervous because he micromanaged. But there was something else. "The thought that he would expose me as being bad and wrong kept creeping into my mind," Esther said.

We used EFT to lower the intensity of emotions that she still felt about losing her last job. As homework, I asked Esther to identify other times in her life where this dynamic had played out. The next week, she said she'd found a distinct pattern in her job experiences. They were all the same: aggressive male managers combined with the fear of being exposed as bad or wrong. We spent that session working through some of the most painful of those memories. Then I asked a series of questions to find the earliest memories connected to the pattern.

Esther said she'd been abused by her rabbi when she was in elementary school. He told her that no one would believe her if she talked about the abuse, because he was held in such high regard in their small orthodox Jewish community. He made her feel responsible for "turning him on," implying that she was inherently bad and wrong.

We tapped the intensity out of all those memories, and a few months later, Esther emailed me to say that she'd landed an ideal job. She was sure that, even if she ended up with a disagreeable male boss, she'd still feel confident and safe.

Esther came to see me because of an issue that limited her, and she wanted to remove the obstacles that prevented her from achieving her career goals. Neither one of us could have guessed where we'd wind up in the process of tapping. But we kept at it until we reached the healing that I knew awaited her.

What to do if tapping takes you somewhere unexpected

It's rare that a presenting issue such as "I can't drive a car," leads to a cause as obvious as, "and I haven't been able to since I was in that accident." My clients and I usually have no idea where we'll end up once we start tapping. In Esther's case, tapping on the pain caused by her most recent job loss brought up a pattern. Tapping on specific memories of previous job losses revealed her memory of her abuse. And tapping on *that* finally eliminated the root cause of her issue and freed her to succeed in her next job.

If you're afraid to begin tapping because you're worried about what might turn up, make that worry the first thing you tackle when you learn how to tap in the next chapter. And know that anytime you need help, you can enlist the aid of an EFT practitioner to get you past any rough spots you may experience.

Are you ready? Let's tap!

CHAPTER 8

HOW TO TAP— LEARNING THE BASICS

Do you remember trying to pat your head and rub your stomach at the same time as a kid? It was probably kind of hard at first, but after a bit of practice, you got the hang of it. EFT is like that. The "head-patting" part is learning how to tap on the right acupoints, and the "stomach-rubbing" part is what you say while you do it. I'll walk you through it here, but if you learn better by watching someone demonstrate, there's also a video tutorial on my website at tapyourpower.net/book.

Although EFT isn't complicated, you'll be more successful if you approach it with a sense of adventure and curiosity. Above all, successful EFT practitioners are detectives who love to solve mysteries. They aren't satisfied by treating only the symptoms of emotional or physical discomfort. They seek and address the root cause.

The term Emotional Freedom Techniques is plural because there are many techniques within EFT. Here, we'll focus on the short formula, which can yield powerful results. You'll get the hang of it in no time!

A precaution

When I first started doing EFT with friends, I was surprised by how often tapping on symptoms led to a memory of childhood sexual abuse. Please don't start tapping on specific issues until you've also read Chapter 9. It provides information about what to do if you feel overwhelmed by anything you unearth during the EFT process. Chapter 5 describes the types of circumstances in which it's best to work with a licensed mental health care professional.

Overview

The following is an overview of the basic EFT formula. You'll find more information about each of these steps later in this chapter.

1. CREATING THE SETUP STATEMENT

- Past: The time the big kids pushed you into the lake, even though you couldn't swim.

    Present: The headache you have right now

    Future: The job interview you'll have next Tuesday.

- Identify the emotion you feel when you think about this event or condition. Let's say you feel *nervous* about your upcoming job interview.

- Rate the intensity level of that emotion using a scale of zero to 10 (where 10 is the highest intensity and zero is none at all) or a scale of low, medium, or high. Let's say you use the former scale and the intensity of your nervousness is a 7.

- Determine whether you feel the emotion anywhere in your body. Let's say you feel it in the pit of your stomach.

- Create a setup statement, which goes something like this: "Even though I feel _____ (emotion) in my ____ (body part where you feel it) about _____ (event or condition), I deeply and completely accept myself." For example, "Even though I feel nervousness in the pit of my stomach about my job interview on Tuesday, I deeply and completely accept myself."

2. CREATING THE REMINDER PHRASE

- Create a reminder phrase, which goes something like this: "This _____ (emotion) in my _____ (body part where you feel it)." For example, "This nervousness in the pit of my stomach."

3. TAPPING

- Say your setup statement out loud three times while tapping the Side of Hand point (illustrated later in this chapter).

- Tap acupoints on your head and upper body while saying the reminder phrase (illustrated later in this chapter).

4. RE-RATING AND REPEATING

- Re-assess the intensity level and compare it to where you were when you started.

- Repeat this process as necessary until you get to an intensity of zero.

Download the journal template

Take a moment now to download and print the journal template at tapyourpower.net/book, so you can fill it out while you read the rest of this chapter. Trust me on this. It'll make EFT a whole lot easier to learn.

What to say when you do EFT

This is the "rubbing your stomach" part of the basic EFT formula. You'll learn how to "pat your head" later in this chapter.

CREATING YOUR SETUP STATEMENT
Five Ws and an H

EFT works on past, current, and future events and conditions. You may consider it odd to tap on something that hasn't happened yet, but future events, like an upcoming surgery or the impending death of a terminally ill loved one, can cause negative emotions right now. You can also experience negative emotions around positive upcoming events, such as a wedding or the birth of a child. If you choose a future scenario, get as specific as you can about the source of your discomfort and imagine it in as much detail as possible. The more focused your setup statement is, the better. Although you don't have to answer all of the following questions, the more you can answer, the more focused your setup statement will be.

- What happened (or will happen)?

- Who was (or will be) involved?

- When did (or will) the event or condition take place?

- Where did (or will) the event or condition take place?

- Why did (or will) the event or condition take place?

- How did (or will) the event or condition take place?

This is the step that people get wrong most often. Very effective EFT focuses on a single, specific event. An example of an unfocused statement is: "The time my brother bugged me." A focused statement is: "The time my brother sat on me at the church picnic and made me cry when I was five." In the latter statement, we have a who (my brother), a where (the church picnic), and a when (at the age of five). A focused statement brings a far clearer image to mind, and the clearer the image you hold, the more effective tapping will be.

Identifying your emotions

Putting your feelings into words can be surprisingly difficult. When we acquire language, concrete words like dog, tree, and ball come first. We need words like these to navigate our physical world (and to tell Mom we want more juice). Abstract words come later, if ever. Adults can easily tell children "that's an apple," because it's something they can be sure of. It's more difficult for them to say something like, "that's guilt," because they can't be sure it's the emotion a child is feeling.

Again, the more specific the description of your feelings, the better. Your downloaded journal template will help you name your emotions.

Identifying where you feel the emotion in your body

Now that you've identified your emotion, take an internal inventory of your body, and see if it's showing up as tension, pressure, constriction, tightness, or another sensation. If so, where? Can you describe the sensation? If you don't sense an emotion in your body, skip this step. Your template includes the illustration below, which you can mark to pinpoint the location of the emotion in your body.

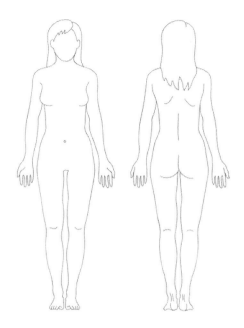

Rating the intensity

On a scale of zero to 10, just how intense is the emotion you're feeling? Your template includes the scale below, which you can mark to identify the intensity of your feelings.

If you find the zero to 10 scale too specific, try rating the intensity at low, medium, or high. Your template includes the scale below. You can draw a needle on it to show the intensity of your feelings.

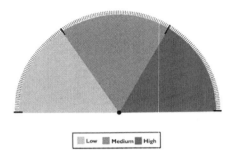

Low Medium High

Putting it all together

Now, use the information in this section to craft your setup statement. This is simply an acknowledgement of what you're feeling and an affirmation of self-acceptance. The first half of the setup statement is the phrase "Even though I feel _____(emotion) in my ____(body part where you feel it) about _____ (event)." The second half is "I deeply and completely accept myself." Put together it might look sound like this: "Even though I feel anger (emotion) in my chest (body part where you feel it) because I found porn on my husband's computer (event), I deeply and completely accept myself." If you can't detect a physical sensation in your body that's related to your emotion, just leave that part out. For example: "Even though I feel anger (emotion) about finding porn on my husband's computer (event), I deeply and completely accept myself."

Creating your reminder phrase

Next, you'll craft a very simple reminder phrase to keep your mind focused on what you're working on. The best way to create it is to use the emotion and the place in your body where you feel it (if you do). For the example above, the reminder phrase would be, "This anger (emotion) in my chest (body part)" or simply, "This anger (emotion)."

You'll be saying this phrase once at each of the points you tap, beginning at the eyebrow, so the phrase needs to be short.

WHAT TO DO WHILE YOU'RE SAYING YOUR SETUP STATEMENT AND REMINDER PHRASE

Now that you know what to say (the "rubbing your stomach" part of this formula), let's learn what to do while you say it. This is the "patting your head" part.

THE ACUPOINTS

For starters, let's go over the acupoints that we use in EFT. There are hundreds of acupoints all over your body, but when tapping, we focus on the nine illustrated and described below. You can activate these easily by tapping them yourself.

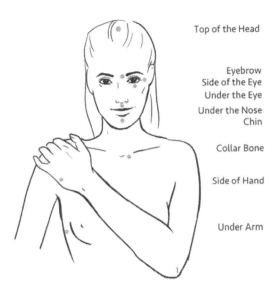

Top of the Head

Eyebrow
Side of the Eye
Under the Eye

Under the Nose
Chin

Collar Bone

Side of Hand

Under Arm

Here are descriptions of acupoint locations in the order in which you'll tap them. Each is followed by an abbreviation that I'll refer to later in this chapter.

1. Side of Hand (SH)
The outer edge of your palm, between the base of your little finger and wrist.

2. Eyebrow (EB)
On the inside of your eyebrow, right where your eyebrow begins.

3. Side of Eye (SE)

On the bony ridge between your eye and your temple. Be gentle with this point. It's a sensitive spot for some people.

4. Under Eye (UE)

On the bone under your eye, in line with your pupil.

5. Under Nose (UN)

Centered between the bottom of the nose and the top of the upper lip.

6. Chin (CH)

Centered between the bottom of the lower lip and the chin.

7. Collarbone (CB)

Locate the U-shaped dip at the top of your sternum (under your Adam's apple), then move down your body an inch and to either side an inch. Because this point is significant, I suggest that you activate both sides at once by making a fist with one hand (to create a larger surface) and gently thump the area where a man would tie a necktie.

8. Under Arm (UA)

About four inches beneath your armpit, where a woman's bra band passes as it wraps around her rib cage.

9. Top of Head (TH)

The very top of your head. If you imagine that you're a marionette, and the top of your head is attached to a cord, you'll easily locate this point.

Tapping FAQ

HOW QUICKLY SHOULD I TAP?

The rate at which you tap is quick, but not rushed. Find a free metronome online (for example, visit a.bestmetronome. com) and set it to 240 beats per minute. That's about right, but it's also OK to go slower, especially as you're learning.

HOW OFTEN SHOULD I TAP EACH POINT?

You'll tap your Side of Hand point continually–as you say your setup statement three times.

You'll tap each of the remaining acupoints while saying your reminder phrase at each point–tapping approximately three to seven times. (Some reminder phrases are longer than others, so you wind up tapping more often when you say those.)

HOW MUCH PRESSURE SHOULD I USE?

Drum your fingertips on a table or desktop. That's about how hard to tap. Harder is *not* better.

HOW IMPORTANT IS IT TO TAP THE *EXACT* LOCATION OF THE ACUPOINT?

Just try to get as close as you can. When you tap, the vibration affects a larger area and is usually enough to activate the point without your needing to be exactly on it.

DOES IT MATTER WHICH EYE I TAP OR WHICH ARM I TAP UNDER?

There are three points around the eye, and it doesn't matter which eye you tap around.

You can tap either underarm point, but again, it's probably most comfortable to use your dominant hand to tap your non-dominant side.

DOES IT MATTER WHICH HAND I USE?

You can use either or both hands. It's usually more comfortable to use your dominant hand to tap your non-dominant side.

You can use both hands to tap the points on your face simultaneously if you like. It's not necessary, but can't hurt.

HOW MANY FINGERS SHOULD I USE?

Using more than one finger gives you a better chance of hitting the acupoint that you're tapping.

The following list is just a summary of what seems to work best. Don't worry about getting the exact number of fingers right for each spot. These are just practical guidelines that will make more sense to you as you gain experience.

When you tap the:

- Side of Hand (SH) point, use four fingers or try tapping both hands against each other at the SH point (this looks like palm-up clapping).

- Top of Head (TOH) point, use four fingers to increase the surface area covered by tapping.

- Points on your face (EB, SE, UE, UN, CH) can't accommodate lots of fingers, so use two (your index and middle finger).

- Collarbone (CB) point, make a fist with one hand (to create a larger surface) and gently thump the area where a man would tie a necktie.

- Underarm (UA) point, use four fingers.

WHAT IF MY EYEGLASSES ARE IN THE WAY? I CAN'T READ THESE DIRECTIONS WITHOUT THEM.

If your glasses get in the way, read and re-read these instructions, then tap along with me in the how- to video on tapyourpower.net/book.

WHY STATE THESE PROBLEMS NEGATIVELY? DOESN'T THAT GO AGAINST THE LAW OF ATTRACTION OR POSITIVE THINKING?

After working with thousands of clients, I believe that positive tapping (as seen in many places on the Internet) can actually do more harm than good because it keeps people in denial. As Carl Jung stated so eloquently, what you resist persists, and denying something doesn't make it go away.

To state that you accept yourself in spite of the negative emotions you feel is a profound and powerful act. Some people say their setup statement once and burst into tears, realizing that their problem isn't what they think it is after all. Their problem is that they judge, and therefore cannot accept themselves for feeling as they do. You're not ruminating on negative emotions while you tap. You're bringing them up for the purpose of neutralizing them.

Practice tapping

Set a metronome if you can, tap a table top or other surface near you to practice the rhythm and rate, than start tapping any spot on your body three to seven times (no need to count). Keep tapping around your body in this way until you feel you've got the hang of it. Try it with two fingers and four fingers, so you can feel the difference in sensation.

Then refer to the section "The acupoints" earlier in this chapter, and try tapping each point in order, beginning with the eyebrow and ending at the top of the head, while maintaining the same rate of speed.

Do this order over and over, until the pressure, pace, and sequence come naturally.

Putting it all together

1. Tap the Side of Hand point while saying your setup statement three times out loud.

2. Tap every acupoint, in order, while saying your reminder phrase at each point.

3. After you tap the top of your head, take a deep breath.

4. Re-rate the intensity of the emotion or sensation that you identified while creating your setup statement.

5. If the intensity is still higher than zero, repeat these steps until your intensity is zero.

Here's how steps one and two above might look, based the example setup statement from earlier in this chapter: "Even though I feel anger in my chest because I found porn on my husband's computer, I deeply and completely accept myself."

Do this	While you say this
Tap the Side of Hand (SH) point	Even though I feel anger in my chest because I found porn on my husband's computer, I deeply and completely accept myself.
	Even though I feel anger in my chest because I found porn on my husband's computer, I deeply and completely accept myself.
	Even though I feel anger in my chest because I found porn on my husband's computer, I deeply and completely accept myself.
Tap the Eyebrow (EB) point	This anger in my chest.
Tap the Side of Eye (SE) point	This anger in my chest.
Tap the Under Eye (UE) point	This anger in my chest.
Tap the Under Nose (UN) point	This anger in my chest.
Tap the Under Chin (CH) point	This anger in my chest.
Tap the Collarbone (CB) point	This anger in my chest.
Tap the Under Arm (UA) point	This anger in my chest.
Tap the Top of the Head (TOH) point	This anger in my chest.

Circle back

Congratulations! Now you know how to tap. Please read the next chapter, then circle back to Chapter 2 to address any issues that prevent you from sharing your needs with your partner or any issues that prevent you from loving your body just as it is. You can also go back to Chapter 3 to address any issues that prevent you from mapping your body's pleasure zones.

CHAPTER 9
CREATING A SAFETY NET WITH EFT

Some days, you might just feel "off," stressed, or emotional without knowing why. Uncomfortable feelings might emerge while you tap. Or you might experience what Daniel Goleman, author of *Emotional Intelligence,* calls an "amygdala hijacking," in which an emotional response seems completely out of proportion to the event that caused it. A quick and effective fix at times like these is to tap while orienting to the here and now.

When you're feeling stirred up, you're usually reliving moments from your past or anticipating things in the future. Orienting EFT can bring you back into the present. We've used it with combat veterans and survivor groups and have found it to be a quick and effective method of self-regulation.

Mark this section of your book and return to it anytime you feel overwhelmed. It will help you re-orient to the here and now.

You'll find the instructions for doing EFT in the previous chapter. Once you're comfortable with the tapping process, you can add Orienting EFT to your toolkit by following the instructions below.

You may find it useful to use your smartphone to record yourself reading the text below, so you can play it back and tap along anytime.

To use Orienting EFT

1. Say each of the following phrases once while tapping your Side of Hand point. Or pick the phrase that feels closest to how you feel right now, and say that three times while tapping your Side of Hand point.

- Even though I've had negative experiences in the past, the truth is that right here, right now, in this moment, I'm perfectly safe.

- Even though I'm noticing some stress and discomfort in my body, and I'm not sure exactly what it's about, I can accept that it's how I'm feeling right now.

- Even though, in this moment, I don't feel anything, in fact I feel kind of numb, I can still bring myself to the present moment.

2. Then say the following phrases while tapping the corresponding acupoints in order:

Eyebrow:	I keep my eyes open with a soft gaze.
Side of Eye:	I look at my surroundings very slowly.
Under Eye:	I allow myself to notice the color, texture, and patterns that surround me.

Under Nose:	I notice variations of shadow and light.
Chin:	I notice small details above, below, and around me.
Collarbone:	I notice the pressure of my feet on the floor.
Under Arm:	I can feel the contact that my body is making with the surface that I'm sitting or standing on.
Top of Head:	I feel the temperature of the air on my skin.
Eyebrow:	I pay attention to the sounds I hear in the background.
Side of Eye	I attend to the timbre and fluctuations in the sound of my voice as I speak.
Under Eye:	I direct my breathing to become slow and rhythmic.
Under Nose:	I determine whether there are on any smells that I can sense around me.
Chin:	I am aware of what time of day it is.
Collarbone:	I'm aware of what month it is.
Under Arm:	I sense a softening of tension throughout my body.
Top of Head:	I feel calm, relaxed, peaceful, settled and in the present moment, where I am perfectly safe.

Continue to tap until any overwhelming emotions or physical sensations subside, and you feel reoriented to the present. If, at any time, you find yourself feeling too overwhelmed to tap, or if you experience significant emotional distress or physical discomfort, stop and seek the services of an appropriate health care professional. If you find yourself overwhelmed often, it may help to engage the services of a professional EFT coach who is qualified to work with your particular issue or a licensed health care professional.

CHAPTER 10
OUCH! OVERCOMING PHYSICAL PAIN OR DISCOMFORT

When I ask clients, "How are you?" at the beginning of sessions, they usually bring up their physical discomforts first. They complain of tension in their shoulders, tiredness, brain fog, cramps, painful periods, headaches, sore throats, congestion, back pain, and other issues. My first questions are always, "Is this something you experience often?" and "Have you seen a doctor?" EFT complements any treatment my clients are already undergoing, but it doesn't *replace* medical or psychological treatment.

When I'm satisfied that clients have addressed their physical conditions medically, we use EFT to bring relief before we delve into any emotional issues they want to address. If they have multiple physical issues, for example, a headache, an upset stomach, *and* a twisted ankle, we start with the issue that's most painful or distracting, and then move on to the next. Addressing physical discomfort first enables clients to feel more relaxed and present during their sessions.

At home, EFT is part of my first aid kit. It's a home remedy that I reach for in the same way that I reach for antibiotic ointment and bandages for cuts, ice for swelling, or salt-water gargles for a sore throat. Here are a few examples of how EFT has helped alleviate pain in friends and family.

- My car door slammed and latched closed on my right hand. The intensity was a 10 on a scale of zero to 10. I got back in the car so people couldn't hear me and literally screamed while I tapped with my left hand. After about five minutes, the pain went away, and there was no bruising afterward.

- On the soccer field, one of my son's teammates twisted an ankle, and with his parents' permission, I tapped to see if his pain would diminish. It did, and he returned to the game.

- On the basketball court, one of my son's teammates was hit in the face with the ball. After his parents and coach attempted to console him for a few minutes, I asked if I could tap to see if it could help him calm down and refocus. It worked, and he, too, returned to the game.

On the other hand, my daughter's friend fell while riding her bike on the street in front of our house and felt a lot of pain in her arm. I did one round of tapping, and when the intensity and location of the pain didn't change, I knew it was time to take her to the emergency room. There, we discovered that her arm was actually broken. Tapping will never replace an x-ray and a cast!

Preparing to tap

For physical pain, we use a technique called "chasing the pain" (Craig, Chasing the Pain - Deeper EFT Relief) or "chasing the sensation." After you've mastered the instructions in Chapter 8, you can customize them to relieve physical pain by applying the information in this chapter.

The following sections will help you make tapping more focused and effective, and therefore more likely to relieve your pain. You wouldn't take your car to the mechanic, simply say "It sounds funny," and expect to get it repaired. Your mechanic is going to ask all kinds of questions that will help him pinpoint and fix the problem. Similarly, tapping is more likely to relieve your pain if you ask yourself a few questions and use your answers as you tap.

Download and print the tapping template at tapyourpower. net/book, so you can fill it out as you answer the questions below.

Where's the pain?

It's important to zoom in on your pain and describe its location in as much detail as possible. For example, "knee" is a location, and "under the patella on the outer side of my left knee" is a *specific* location.

Your tapping template includes the illustration below, so you can circle, color, or draw an arrow to the area that hurts.

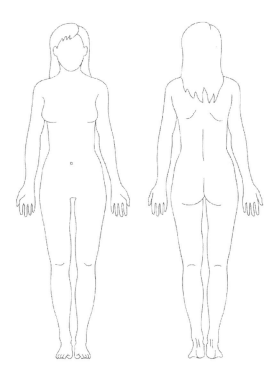

WHAT SIZE IS THE PAIN?

We tend to generalize pain, but it's unlikely that your *whole* body hurts. Find the edges of your pain. If you have trouble, it might be easier to identify what *doesn't* hurt and work your way in.

How big is the painful area? What shape is it? Is it flat or three-dimensional?

WHAT'S THE QUALITY OF THE PAIN?

There are different types of pain, for example: throbbing, radiating, dull, or piercing. Try to describe the quality of the pain on your own. If you find that difficult, and many do, the following list may help:

- Achy, sore, bruised

- Congested

- Contracted

- Cramped, constricted

- Deep, penetrating

- Dull

- Gnawing

- Heavy, dense, dark

- Hot, burning

- Itchy

- Jumping, twitchy

- Knotted

- Nauseous, queasy, churning

- Nervy, buzzy, electric

- Numb, wooden, disconnected

- Pinching

- Pressing, squeezing, crushing, suffocating

- Prickly

- Pulling, tugging

- Radiating, shooting

- Raw

- Shaky, shivery, trembly

- Stabbing, piercing, sharp, stinging

- Stiff, stuck, frozen, jammed

- Tearing

- Tender, sensitive

- Throbbing, pulsing, pounding

- Tight, tense, clenched

- Twisted, wrenching

HOW INTENSE IS THE PAIN?

Rate the intensity of your pain on a scale of zero to 10 (where 10 is the highest intensity and zero is none at all). Or use a scale of low, medium, or high.

Your template includes both types of scales, so you can mark them to indicate the intensity of your pain.

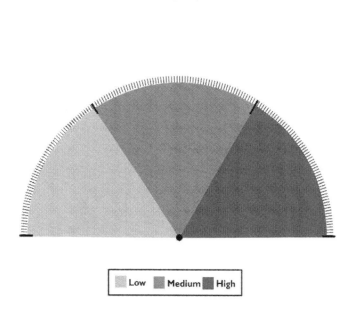

Low   Medium   High

Tapping to relieve pain

Now that you've answered all these questions, you're ready
to tap.

CREATING YOUR SETUP STATEMENT

Using the information that you gathered, construct a setup statement by providing the missing information below.

Even though I have this (size)_____(quality) _____ pain in my (location) _____I deeply and completely accept myself.

For example: Even though I have this pear-sized hot pain in my uterus, I deeply and completely accept myself.

THE REMINDER PHRASE

Construct a reminder phrase by filling in the missing information below:

This (size) _____(quality) _____ pain in my (location)_____.

For example: This pear-sized hot pain in my uterus.

PUTTING IT ALL TOGETHER AND TAPPING

Based on the example we've been using throughout this chapter, a round of tapping would look like this:

Do this	While you say this
Tap the Side of Hand (SH) point	Even though I have this pear-sized hot pain in my uterus, I deeply and completely accept myself. Even though I have this pear-sized hot pain in my uterus, I deeply and completely accept myself. Even though I have this pear-sized hot pain in my uterus, I deeply and completely accept myself.
Tap the Eyebrow (EB) point	This pear-sized hot pain in my uterus.
Tap the Side of Eye (SE) point	This pear-sized hot pain in my uterus.
Tap the Under Eye (UE) point	This pear-sized hot pain in my uterus.
Tap the Under Nose (UN) point	This pear-sized hot pain in my uterus.
Tap the Under Chin (CH) point	This pear-sized hot pain in my uterus.
Tap the Collarbone (CB) point	This pear-sized hot pain in my uterus.
Tap the Under Arm (UA) point	This pear-sized hot pain in my uterus.
Tap the Top of the Head (TOH) point	This pear-sized hot pain in my uterus.

If you need a refresher on tapping, see Chapter 8.

RE-RATE THE INTENSITY

After you've finished the first round of tapping, notice whether anything has changed. Did the location of your pain change? The quality? The intensity?

If the only thing that changed was the intensity, do another round of tapping using the same setup statement and reminder phrase. If the intensity continues to diminish, and the location and quality remain the same, repeat rounds of tapping until the pain abates.

If the quality or location changes, however, update your setup statement and reminder phrase and begin a new round of tapping aimed at the new symptoms. This technique is "called chasing the pain" because the location and quality of pain often changes during a session.

Here's an example from one of my recent workshops. A woman in her forties felt a tightness and burning in her upper thigh that was a 7 in intensity. After one round of tapping, the pain moved to her other thigh. When we tapped on that, it decreased in intensity and stayed put, so we did another round. Then it moved to the back of her neck, where she described it as tension the size of a baseball. We tapped, and the intensity went down even further. Eventually, her pain stopped moving, and the intensity diminished.

What to do if the pain doesn't abate

If, after a number of rounds of tapping, the intensity of your pain doesn't lessen, here are some things to consider:

- You may have a medical problem that EFT can't fix. Assuming that you've already seen a physician, as recommended at the beginning of this chapter, I recommend seeing another and getting a second opinion.

- Your setup and reminder statements may not be specific enough.

- There may be a hidden benefit to your pain. For more information about this, see Chapter 5.

- You may need to be persistent and keep working at it.

- You may benefit from working with an EFT coach.

- Your pain may not go away until you address underlying emotional issues. For more information, see Chapter 11.

In my experience, the last item in this list turns out to be the cause of unresolved pain most of the time. For example, I once had a client who had extremely painful periods. When I asked her how long they'd been that way, she said, "Since the beginning." I asked what it was like when her period started, and she said, "I was in Catholic school. The nuns told me that my womb was weeping because it was barren." We tapped on that memory, and her painful eriods disappeared.

If you uncover a connection like that, it's important not to judge it, even if it doesn't make sense. Connections that seem illogical to us as adults often have their origin in our sense of powerlessness and dependence as children.

Symptoms as metaphors

If you have a	Is
stabbing pain in your back	somebody betraying you or "stabbing you in the back?"
stiff neck	somebody around you being "a pain in the neck?"
headache	somebody "giving you a headache?"
shoulder that hurts when you raise your arm	something out of your reach?
stomach ache	there something in your life you find "hard to digest?"
sore throat	there some news you find "hard to swallow?"

These associations may seem corny, but think about how they came to be part of our vernacular. Is it so surprising that our subconscious minds might alert us to underlying issues by using these familiar metaphors?

CHAPTER 11

HEALING YOUR HEART— OVERCOMING EMOTIONAL PAIN

Have you ever been someplace new, perhaps a shopping mall or a theme park, and tried to get oriented by looking at a displayed map? Nothing really makes sense in that context until you find the big red arrow and the words "You are here."

EFT works the same way. When I ask clients, "How are you?" at the beginning of sessions, and they say "Overwhelmed," "My life sucks," or "I can't believe what I'm going through," that's exactly where we start, even if they intended to work on something entirely different. We start right where they are. Then, like detectives, we follow clues that lead from there.

The setup statements we use incorporate their responses word-for-word (even though some of them aren't very specific):

- Even though I feel overwhelmed...

- Even though my life sucks...

- Even though I can't believe what I'm going through...

We don't move on to what the client came for until the intensity of his or her current feelings goes down to a 3, 2, 1, or zero on a scale of zero to 10.

I began using EFT because I wanted to heal a physical condition. But the more I tapped, the more I realized that I was in denial about my troubled marriage. I was afraid that if I looked at it closely enough, it would result in consequences that I didn't want to deal with. So that's where I started. I tapped about *the fear* I felt about looking at my situation more closely. I don't know if I would've had the courage to dig deeper if I hadn't addressed that fear first.

Starting with how you're feeling *right now* removes obstacles, clears resistance, and helps you get unstuck.

Sometimes, the feelings that clients and I tackle first seem to have nothing at all to do with the issues they came to resolve. Such was the case with Desiree, who came to work with me on problems that had become so troublesome that she decided to "run away" from her home and husband in the Southwest to an island in the Pacific Northwest. Desiree had a full-time job and was caring for two elderly relatives when she discovered that her husband was having an affair. But what she led with one day was: "There are things I'm afraid of that I don't understand. I can't even order a cup of coffee from the local coffee shop."

The owner, it turned out, was bald, and Desiree was terrified of bald men. She avoided being in any situation near them and experienced such overwhelming fear when she saw a bald man in public that she would cross the street to avoid him. To put this in context, 40 percent of men have noticeable hair loss by the age of 35, and by the age of 60, 65 percent do (Statistic Brain Research Institute, 2014), so this fear was very limiting for Desiree.

Fears like that don't happen in a vacuum, so I asked Desiree questions about the nature of the fear. Several events came to mind as we worked on a memory of a family member who was mean and happened to be bald, but then Desiree suddenly remembered a long-buried sexual experience.

When Desiree was six years old, her best friend Dolores lived up the hill. Being in the same neighborhood, Desiree played with Dolores frequently, and many times, the play dates took place at Dolores' home. One day, Dolores' older brother recruited the girls to go down to the basement and play doctor with him. He asked Desiree to lie down while he "examined" her, and Dolores lay beside her holding her hand during this exploration. Desiree remembers it "feeling good." There was not much more to the event.

But Desiree's mother somehow found out that her daughter had been playing doctor. Very little was explained to Desiree, but from then on, she was no longer allowed to play with her friend, and soon afterward, Dolores' family moved out of town. Desiree came to believe that what she'd done was horribly wrong, that the feelings she had during the experience were bad, and that she'd been the cause of her friend's move. From that point on, Desiree's mother became so overprotective that Desiree was never allowed to spend the night anywhere other than her own home, including her grandparents' house. It wasn't Desiree's experience of playing doctor that traumatized Desiree. It was her mother's draconian reaction to it.

What does all this have to do with a fear of bald men? In the basement, where the "doctor" examined his patients, there was a toy shelf filled with dolls and games. On the top shelf was a figurine of a clown who had Bozo-like hair: bald on top and long on the sides.

Over a series of a few weekly EFT sessions, Desiree was able to release the guilt she felt about what had happened, as well as her fear of bald men. We tested the work we had done by recalling the events once more, and asking Desiree to try to bring up any negative emotion as she talked in great detail about what had happened. Her final test was walking into a store that had a bald, male employee. She was delighted when she was able to go right up to him and have a normal, casual conversation without any fear whatsoever.

Once our work was complete, Desiree went back to her home in the Southwest. She found that everything had changed for her, including her marriage. More than a year later, I checked in on her to see how she was doing, and she said, "It's amazing. Sometimes I still can't believe how much I've changed. There's no shield, I've opened up so much. Sex is better than it's ever been, and I'm not afraid of life any more. My life had become so small without my becoming aware of it, and I wouldn't be this happy or free without EFT."

Start where you are

Not sure where to start with EFT? Start with how you feel right now. Consider each of the following questions. Name the emotions that you have in response to each one and then, on a scale of zero to 10 (or low, medium, high), rate the intensity of each emotion.

- How do you feel about your physical health?

- How do you feel about your appearance?

- How do you feel about your romantic relationship?

- How do you feel about your sex life?

- How do you feel about your future with your partner?

- How do you feel about the possibility of your future without a partner?

- How do you feel about using EFT for your own sexual healing?

If any of the emotions you're feeling have an intensity of 5 or greater on a scale of zero to 10, or an intensity of medium on the low-medium-high scale, tap until the intensity goes down to a 3 or lower (or low on the low-medium-high scale).

The root of pain and discomfort

EFT is based on the assumption that physical and emotional pain and discomfort is rooted in unreleased negative emotions, and I've found that to be true in my practice. Usually, the search for the cause of our pain and discomfort doesn't lead where we expect–as was the case with Desiree. It seems utterly illogical that her fear of bald men could be connected to a clown doll she'd seen once in her childhood, but after we tapped on that memory, her fear disappeared.

While exploring, it's critical that you welcome all emotions and become curious about the messages they bear. Every single one of them is important. In fact, if you had to guess, which women do you think are more likely to get breast cancer: those who express anger or those who don't? Turns out the characteristic shared by the most breast cancer patients involved in a 1974 study was the suppression of anger. The authors of the study wrote, "Our principal finding was a significant association between the diagnosis of breast cancer and a behavior pattern, persisting throughout adult life, of abnormal release of emotions. This abnormality was, in most cases, extreme suppression of anger and, in patients over 40, extreme suppression of other feelings."

But the opposite end of the emotional spectrum also turned out to be a risk factor. "Extreme expression of emotions, though much less common, also occurred in a higher proportion of cancer patients than controls," the authors of the study wrote. (Greer & Morris, 1975)

My wish for you is that, through your knowledge of EFT, you find the courage to live life more fully. Whenever you find that the emotions you're feeling are too intense or overwhelming, use EFT as your safety net.

CHAPTER 12
EMOTIONAL SPRING CLEANING

Most of my clients and students communicate with me via the Internet, often via videoconferencing, so the computer in my home office has to work reliably, and my Internet connection has to be stable and fast. We were having trouble with that part, so we switched from DSL to cable, but after the installation technician left the first time, the Internet stopped working. He came back and swapped out the router on his second visit, but the signal was weak, so he installed a range extender. That still didn't provide a consistent Internet connection, so on the third visit, he rewired the attic. Now, the Internet is finally fast and reliable throughout the house.

Using EFT requires a similar process of elimination. Most of the time, clients come to me with specific symptoms that they want relief from, and neither of us knows exactly what's causing them. They may have a hunch, but often it's something deeper. After I ask a bunch of questions, tapping itself often brings more clarity, and we usually figure it out together.

Most of the time, people use EFT to address specific problems or symptoms. But what if your goal isn't specific? What if it's broad, like achieving inner peace? That, too, is possible using EFT. It's called the "Personal Peace Procedure," and the goal is deep, abiding, unshakable peace.

The Personal Peace Procedure

When I did the Personal Peace Procedure myself, it felt like a weight I didn't even know existed had been lifted off my shoulders. It made me more resilient. I was no longer as easily triggered as I had been in the past, and I was able to be more present than I was before.

If you could have a conversation about water with a fish, it wouldn't be a very long one. Fish don't know they're swimming in water. Without a contrast (like air) it would be difficult to explain to them what water is. Before I did the Personal Peace Procedure, the water I was swimming in was made up of loneliness, frustration, and fear of change. *I had no contrast*. I had forgotten what it was like *not* to feel those things. After I did the Personal Peace Procedure, peace became the water I swam in, and when something made that water turbulent, it stood out in a way that made me address it. I had a contrast again. If the situations and people I was working with didn't serve my highest and best interests, they had to get out of the water.

Saying "I deeply and completely accept myself" so many times in the process of tapping helped me to truly accept myself. It became easier to take steps that were aligned with that self-acceptance—even when they were difficult. In my case, it meant ending my marriage to the father of my children. Self-acceptance meant not allowing myself to be treated in unloving ways. It meant eliminating obstacles that prevented me from expressing my true self and following my passions.

The Personal Peace Procedure takes time and effort, but it's well worth it. Here's how to do it.

STEP 1: MAKE YOUR LIST

It all starts with a list. You can categorize your list chronologically, by people, or by places. Then underneath each category, list as many events and experiences as you can think of *that you wish you could've skipped*. This list should contain at least 100 items. (Mine contained about 150.) Include everything you wish you could've skipped, even things you think you've put behind you. This list should span your *entire life*.

Don't try to create the list in one sitting. Set a deadline a week from now, and work on it a day at a time, finishing the list by your deadline.

Creating a chronological list

If you're organizing your list chronologically, it might look something like this:

Preschool

- Throwing up in the classroom

- And so on

Kindergarten

- Breaking my arm when I fell off the slide

- And so on

First grade

- Mom and Dad got divorced

- And so on

Creating a list organized by people

If you prefer, you can create a list that's organized by the people who played a major role in your life. Your list might look something like this:

Mom

- Having to wear the clothes that mom sewed herself to school

And so on

- Dad

- Having to pull my pants down for spankings

- And so on

Sister

- Ruby flirted my boyfriend away from me

- And so on

Creating a list organized by places

If you remember things best by location, this type of organization might work better for you. Create a section for each significant place that you've lived or been in. Your list might look something like this.

Texas

- Dad spent a year away from us while stationed in Asia with the Air Force.

- And so on

Illinois

- I fell and hit my head on the concrete steps in front of the house.

- And so on

Virginia

- Grandpa died.

- And so on

Tools for list-making

I recommend that you purchase a blank journal, divide it into sections that correspond to how you're organizing your list, and then create your list section by section. Leave a few blank lines between each item in your list, so you can write notes. And leave some room at the end of each list, in case you remember additional events later.

For example, if you choose to categorize your list by people who played a major role in your life, you might title the first section "Mom," the next section, "Dad," and so on. Leave a few blank pages at the end of each section, in case memories arise as you work through other sections.

Another way to organize your list is to purchase a three-ring binder with as many tabbed dividers as you have categories. For example, if you're categorizing your list by place, you might have a tab for Texas, one for Illinois, one for Virginia, and so on. Then print out a bunch of journal templates at tapyourpower.net/book and fill out one template for each item in your list. This method is more guided and thorough.

STEP 2: ASSESS THE INTENSITY OF EACH ITEM IN YOUR LIST

After you've created your list, go through it from beginning to end and assess the intensity of your feelings when you recall each event. Again, this isn't something you can do in one sitting. Give yourself a week or so.

This step is very important. *Do not skip it!* (You'll find out why later in this chapter.) You can use one of two methods to assess the intensity your emotions, just be sure you use the same one throughout the entire process.

The zero-to-ten scale

On a zero-to-ten scale, identify how intense your emotions are when you think about each item in your list, and write that number beside each item. Zero is no intensity at all, and ten is the maximum intensity.

A chronological list with intensity ratings might look something like this:

Preschool

- Throwing up in the classroom (6)

- And so on

Kindergarten

- Breaking my arm when I fell off the slide (8)

- And so on

First grade

- Mom and Dad got divorced (10)

- And so on

The low/medium/high scale

If a zero-to-ten scale doesn't feel right to you, try a low/medium/high scale instead. Rate the intensity of the emotions you feel about each item on your list, and then write it down beside each item. A list organized by significant people using low/medium/high ratings would look something like this:

Mom

- Having to wear clothes to school that mom sewed herself (low)

- And so on

Dad

- Having to pull my pants down for spankings (high)

- And so on

Sister

- Ruby flirted my boyfriend away from me (medium)

- And so on

STEP 3: TAP ON ONE OR TWO ITEMS ON YOUR LIST EVERY DAY

Give yourself three months or so to get through the entire Personal Peace Procedure, tapping on one or two items in your list every morning or evening, and no more. As you work, a phenomenon called the "generalization effect" will most likely prevent you from having to tap on every item in your list. This is why including intensity ratings is so important.

You'll find, as you make your way through the list, that some items have completely lost their intensity, and if that happens, you can skip them. This is because many events are connected, and tapping on one event can collapse an entire network. For example, say you've had a number of events in which you froze when getting up to speak in front of people. As you tap on one of these events, you might discover the core issue and collapse all the related events on your list as a result.

For this reason, be sure to double-check your intensity rating before you tap on an issue. If it's zero or low, you can cross it off and move on to the next one.

IF YOU CAN'T GET THE INTENSITY LEVEL DOWN TO ZERO OR LOW

The goal of tapping is to get the intensity to zero or low, depending on the scale you use. When I did the Personal Peace Procedure myself, I wasn't able to get the intensity level down to zero for a few items on my list, and that may happen to you, too. I worked through those items with the help of a professional EFT practitioner and recommend that you do the same. Sometimes you can't "see the forest for the trees," and the perspective of a trained, objective outsider can make all the difference.

A WORD OF CAUTION

Although the Personal Peace Procedure is one of the most empowering ways that I know of to help yourself, there are times when I strongly recommend against going it alone. To identify which events you should tackle only with the help of a professional, see the section titled "When to work with an EFT practitioner" in Chapter 5.

CHAPTER 13
THE POWER OF BELIEF

Many of our behaviors are rooted in beliefs that just don't make sense from a grown-up perspective. Where do they come from, and why do they have such power over our everyday lives? Let's start at the beginning.

"The first six years of a child's life is spent in a hypnotic trance," says Bruce Lipton, author of *The Biology of Belief*. "Its perceptions of the world are directly downloaded into the subconscious during this time, without the discrimination of the, as yet, dormant self-conscious mind. Consequently, our fundamental perceptions about life and our role in it are learned before we express the capacity to choose or reject those beliefs. We were simply 'programmed.'"

When solitude seems life-threatening

Here's an example of such a belief, formed in childhood, that limited one of my adult clients. Yolanda said she was terrified of being alone, an experience she was afraid she might not survive. When I asked her how this currently affected her life, she said that she had yet to confront her current boyfriend, who she knew was cheating on her. She wanted to speak her truth, have an intelligent conversation about it, and then decide if she wanted to leave or stay in the relationship. But she'd rehearsed the talk in her mind hundreds of times, and felt paralyzed by the fear that he might leave her.

We started by tapping on Yolanda's fear. I had her imagine a dialog with her boyfriend, and we tapped on the fears that arose as she did. This brought up several other instances in Yolanda's past when she'd been cheated on. She hadn't been able to confront her previous boyfriend, a sex addict, either. In fact, she said that if he hadn't left her for another woman, she'd still be with him. We tapped on several key events in that relationship.

By the third session, Yolanda and I had established enough rapport that I was able to ask her about her childhood. She told me about going on a vacation in Asia with her mother, father, and younger sibling as a very young girl. There, she saw her parents fight like she'd never seen them fight before. I asked her how her little-girl self felt watching that fight through the open door of an adjoining room, and she said, "She's terrified that they'll abandon her there in a foreign land." We tapped until the intense feelings were gone.

Soon afterward, Yolanda was able to talk to her boyfriend about his infidelity, and they decided to split up. But Yolanda was finally at peace and was learning to enjoy solitude for the first time in her life.

Like most children, Yolanda feared that she wouldn't survive without her parents. But for her, that fear was intensified in a foreign country, where her chances of surviving alone seemed more remote. This is an example of emotional learning, which "usually consists of much more than stored memory of the 'raw data,' of what one's senses were registering and what emotions one was experiencing during an original experience," write Bruce Ecker, Robin Ticic, and Laurel Hulley in *Unlocking the Emotional Brain*. "Also learned—that is, stored in implicit memory—is a constructed *mental model* of how the world functions, a template or schema that is the individual's sense-making generalization of the raw data of perception and emotion. This model is created and stored with no awareness of doing so. It does not exist in words but is no less well-defined or coherent for that. The emotional brain then uses this model or schema for self-protectively *anticipating* similar experiences in the future and recognizing them instantly when they begin (or seem) to occur. Emotional memory converts the past into an expectation of the future, without our awareness...."

The experience Yolanda had on vacation in Asia caused her to create a mental model that she unconsciously applied to her romantic relationships as an adult: "If he leaves me, I won't survive." Through EFT, she was able to make that model conscious and eliminate the "programming" that had driven her choices and behavior for most of her life.

When men seem dangerous

Denia came to me because she couldn't feel anything when having sex with her husband. She described the feeling as "checking out" and said, "I see myself almost floating above my body whenever my husband makes love to me." When I asked if she had always felt this way, she said that it only happened when she was having sex with someone she was in love with. It didn't happen in the past, when she'd had casual flings or one-night stands.

I had her imagine that she was in bed with her husband, and he suddenly initiated sex. Even envisioning it made her feel checked out, so we tapped on that, using the setup statement, "Even though I feel checked out of my body when Hans starts kissing me, I deeply and completely accept myself." The intensity began to decrease, but then another memory surfaced.

When Denia was 10 and alone at home, she found a pornographic magazine in the drawer of her father's nightstand. The magazine contained images of bondage, with women in the submissive role, that Denia found disturbing and repulsive–but she also found a few of the images stimulating.

We tapped on the images and how they made Denia feel. "That was the day I decided that all men are dangerous," she said. Looking back on her sexual history, Denia was surprised to realize that she checked out with her husband, whom she loved and generally felt safe with, but felt excited by risky sex with virtual strangers.

After we cleared the belief that men are dangerous, Denia reported that she was enjoying a fulfilling sex life with her husband–for which she was able to be fully present.

What are your limiting beliefs?

Here are some beliefs that regularly come up in my practice. If some of these feel true for you, you can clear them by following the procedure in the next section.

Belief	What I find in my practice
The world is a dangerous place (Otherwise things like this don't happen).	This often manifests itself as allergies or food sensitivities, which seem to clear up at the same time the limiting belief does. It also often manifests itself as obesity, because weight forms a shield that protects people from unwanted advances. People who have experienced physical or sexual abuse often hold this belief.
I must be in control at all times (Otherwise something similar will happen again).	This often manifests itself in an inability to have orgasms. These people's need to be in control is often the result of chaotic childhoods in which there was little order, rhythm, or structure.
My body betrayed me (It felt good to have this go on even when my mind told me it shouldn't).	If sex didn't feel good, our species wouldn't have survived, and even in the context of abuse or rape, victims sometimes feel pleasurable sensations. This is understandably difficult for people to reconcile.

I am bad (I must have done something to bring this on).	People who hold this belief have trouble asking for what they want, either in a relationship or in bed, because they feel they don't deserve it in some way.
I am powerless, weak, or not smart enough (I couldn't stop it from happening).	Lacking self-confidence, these people, however talented they may be, don't pursue their dreams.
There must be something wrong with me/I am different/weird (No one else has gone through this).	People who hold this belief often find it difficult to connect with others, because they're afraid others will reject or judge them when they find out the "truth."
I have to play small (Getting attention is dangerous).	In business, these people have a hard time hanging up a shingle and promoting themselves. In relationships, they put the needs of others before their own, and can't ask for or receive what they want.
I am a sinner/evil (Pious people don't have this happen).	People who have been abused, particularly in religious families, often feel this way.

If you find that you hold some of these, please don't judge yourself. You didn't consciously *choose* these beliefs. They're the subconscious conclusions you drew in response to life events that most likely took place at a very young age.

The following list contains additional limiting beliefs from Karl Dawson and Kate Marillat's *Transform Your Beliefs, Transform Your Life: EFT Tapping Using Matrix Reimprinting*. Go through the preceding list and the one below, and note which beliefs feel true for you. Then tap on them by following the procedure in next section.

- I'm not good enough.

- I'm not loveable.

- The world is a dangerous place.

- I'm worthless.

- I'm incapable.

- I'm misunderstood.

- I'm abandoned.

- I'm betrayed.

- I'm unattractive.

- I'm unproductive.

- I'm incompetent.

- I'm a failure.

- I'm a victim.

- I'm a burden.

- I'm dumb.

- I'm always used.

- I'm alone.

- I'm bad.

- I'm guilty.

- I'm sinful.

- I'm confused.

- I'm trapped.

- I'm powerless.

- I'm inferior.

- I'm separated from God

Clearing limiting beliefs with EFT

Before using EFT to clear a limiting belief, make sure you've mastered tapping by reading Chapter 8. Then follow these steps:

1. Identify the belief that you want to clear, and then say it out loud.

2. Instead of rating the belief on an intensity scale of zero to 10 (or low-medium-high) as you've done so far, rate it on a scale of zero to 100 percent *true for you* on an emotional level.

3. Ask yourself "How is this belief showing up in my life today?" Think of a specific example. (You'll find some in the table above.)

4. What feelings arise for you when you think of that example?

5. Rate those feelings on an intensity scale of zero to 10 (or low-medium-high).

6. Then tap, as described in Chapter 8.

Tabletops and table legs

Usually, my clients come with one big issue that they want help with. EFT founder Gary Craig called this the "tabletop." He called the contributing causes "table legs." In my experience, you don't have to eliminate every leg for the entire table to come crashing down.

Here's an example from my practice. Starr wanted to explore the possibility that her digestive issues, which included sensitivities to gluten and dairy products, may have emotional causes. When I work with clients who suffer from allergies, I often bring the substance that they're allergic to in a container, to see how they react to its presence emotionally. In Starr's case, I brought a piece of bread, to which she responded with fear.

When I brought Starr's attention to how she reacted *emotionally* to the bread, she realized that she was sending a powerful message to her body–before the bread even came *near* her! Was Starr's digestive system reacting to *gluten* or to *fear*?

Starr and I started tapping on her fear. After I few rounds of tapping, her fear subsided (table leg number one), but Starr realized she often felt exactly the same way when her partner, Joe, initiated sex. "This darkness falls on me sometimes when he initiates sex," she said.

I asked her what, specifically, she found upsetting about Joe's sexual advances, and she recounted that his touching her breasts or genitals didn't bother her. But if he looked at or touched her bottom, she became upset. I asked her why, and she responded that she'd always hated the way her rear end looked. We tapped until she felt okay about it.

The next time I saw her, Starr mentioned that a few memories had surfaced that she had tapped on herself. Several went back to childhood, when kids at school had teased her about having a "bubble butt." I tested to see if she was completely clear of those events, and we tapped on one or two remaining issues. (Table leg number two.)

There may have been other contributing causes to Starr's digestive issues, but kicking two "legs" out from under her "table" caused it to collapse completely. A month later, she wrote to say that she was now enjoying pizza *as well as* great sex, which included enjoying Joe's touch on her rear end.

If you need help

Although my goal in writing this book is to empower you to heal yourself, we all have blind spots and can sometimes benefit from the help of others. *Seventy percent* of my clients are practicing EFT professionals. They come to me because I can help them see what they can't. And when I'm too close to my own forest to see the trees, I engage the help of other EFT professionals myself. After all, dentists don't give themselves root canals.

There's a technique, called Matrix Reimprinting, that's beyond the scope of this book, but I've found it especially helpful in clearing limiting beliefs. Although EFT can help take the "charge" out of negative memories, the memories themselves don't change. Matrix Reimprinting engages your imagination and helps you transform your memories. It enables you to become your own superhero and do what you wish you'd done, get the help you wish you'd had, and bring in the resources you wish you could've accessed at the time.

Although you can learn to do Matrix Reimprinting on your own, just like EFT, it's a bit harder to do for yourself. If you need help, I'd be happy to work with you, or refer you to someone whose work I respect. You can make an appointment or contact me via my website at tapyourpower.net. Note that geographic proximity is no problem: I do most of my work via Skype and have clients around the globe.

CHAPTER 14
THE MIND-BODY CONNECTION

The longer I practice EFT, the more I wonder how we ever embraced Cartesian dualism. In the 17th century, philosopher Rene Descartes promoted a worldview in which the mind and body were considered distinctly separate. Until that time, the prevalent Christian view was that, to ascend into heaven, the human body had to be kept intact. Therefore, studying the body via dissection was prohibited. The benefit of the Cartesian model was that separating body from soul made the body available to science, and that led to a boom in scientific disciplines and discoveries. (Mehta, 2011)

But science itself has proven the separation of mind and body to be untrue. For example, a recent study shows that meditation and participation in support groups benefits breast cancer patients on a cellular level. (Carlson, et al., 2015) My clients and students have shown me over and over again how inseparable the mind and body truly are. In fact, EFT itself is based on the assumption that physical issues are strongly influenced, and sometimes even caused by unresolved emotional issues.

Illness, pain, or discomfort are ways that our bodies can get our attention. The mistake we've made for most of our lives is that we've reached for ibuprofen, an ice pack, antacids, or anything that brings relief of our symptoms without asking some important questions first.

Sometimes, when tapping for a physical issue comes to a plateau, pain or discomfort persists, and additional rounds of tapping no longer lower the intensity, I ask my clients the following questions. These questions help us find the memories or emotions that are at the root of the physical condition, so we can address the cause instead of the symptoms.

When did it start?

People often miss the connection between the onset of their symptoms and what was transpiring in their lives when those symptoms began. What happened around the time when your symptoms started? How did you feel about it? Tap on any negative memories that come up for you.

What was happening in your life six months to a year before it started?

The onset of symptoms isn't always immediate. What happened *before* the onset of your condition? It's worth tapping on negative memories of events that took place within a year of the onset of your symptoms, even if they turn out to be unrelated.

What could this be a metaphor for?

Is your sore throat a metaphor for holding back your truth? Is your backache a metaphor for a burden that's too heavy to carry alone? Is your stomachache a metaphor for hating someone's guts? You'll find a few other metaphors in Chapter 10.

If your body was sending you a message, what might it be saying?

I've had clients whose symptoms abate on Friday and resume again on Monday, and it doesn't take much effort to conclude that their symptoms are work-related. If you're having symptoms, such as a headache, on work days, but not on the weekend, what could be causing them? It could be anything from ethical quandaries over covering up your boss's affair to your cube-mate's perfume. Tap on *that* before reaching for a pain reliever.

What is your physical condition saying (to yourself or others) that you couldn't say yourself?

Sometimes our bodies draw boundaries that we have trouble drawing for ourselves. For example, say you don't want to have sex with your partner, but don't want to hurt his feelings by telling him so. Prolonged and painful periods make that conversation less necessary. Is your condition sending a message that you're uncomfortable putting into words? Or is it getting you attention that you can't ask for directly?

How do you feel about your condition? What else do you feel that way about?

In an example in the previous chapter, Starr realized that the fear she felt about a piece of bread (which had historically affected her digestive system adversely) was similar to the fear she sometimes felt when her partner initiated sex. That enabled us to address both issues while tapping. What do your feelings about your condition remind you of? What are they similar to?

What makes your condition better? What makes it worse?

If walking backward makes your leg hurt less, but walking forward makes it hurt more, is there something "before you" that you'd rather avoid? Think about what aggravates and improves your condition, and see if it leads to an *Aha*!

Be playful and curious in your questioning. No association, no metaphor is too ludicrous to follow up on.

Here's a mind-body example from my practice. Leslie came in for help with her debilitating uterine fibroids, which are a type of benign tumor that's fairly common in menstruating women. Although fibroids can be painless for many, in Leslie's case, they led to prolonged, heavy menstrual periods lasting 10 to 12 days. They also caused her to feel excruciating pain in her lower abdomen three weeks a month. She couldn't engage in sexual activity during that time because she found penetration unbearable. She'd worked with half a dozen physicians on her symptoms, and when I saw her, she was working with a doctor who was helping her with hormone therapy and nutrition.

Leslie and I started by addressing the deep sadness and hopelessness she felt about her situation. She'd experienced painful periods since her twenties. Now, at age 32, they were worse than ever. During our second session, I asked Leslie if she could make a connection between the time they started becoming painful and a change in her life circumstances. After a few moments, she said that she'd never made the connection before, but that they did seem to start getting worse after she got married.

Leslie had waited until after her wedding to have intercourse for the first time and prepared herself for her wedding night by studying books on sex. She believed strongly in saving herself for her beloved and was curious, excited, and nervous about her first sexual experience.

She went into the bathroom of their honeymoon suite to slip on a seductive nightgown, but by the time she returned, her husband, who'd become intoxicated during the reception, had passed out. From that moment on, Leslie felt disappointed by her lackluster sex life. Her husband, though a wonderful partner in other ways, was an uneducated lover.

We spent time tapping on specific aspects of Leslie's honeymoon experience, as well as other times that led Leslie to conclude that sex was only for a man's enjoyment. During our next session, Leslie and I worked on her fears and the shame she felt at the mere thought of discussing the situation with her husband. By the end, she was confident that an open and honest conversation with her husband would actually help the situation.

A week later, a glowing Leslie returned to my office. Her husband had indeed been receptive to learning more about pleasuring her. Soon afterward, Leslie experienced her first orgasm. When her period came a few weeks later, she was in complete shock that she felt no pain, and her bleeding was back to a manageable level.

The body remembers

Leslie was able to recall memories that contributed to her condition, but that's not always the case. In her book titled *The Body Remembers: The Psychophysiology of Trauma and Trauma Treatment*, author Babette Rothschild helps us understand why the body often "remembers" what the mind cannot:

- We can't recall events that occurred before our limbic

systems (the part of our brain that plays a role in forming memories) have developed. That usually occurs by age two.

- In addition to the fight or flight response, we have a survival strategy called the freeze response. It can be difficult to remember what occurs during freeze, which is a response that automatically takes place when neither fight nor flight are feasible. The freeze response is involuntary and numbs us to physical and psychological pain. This numbing is called dissociation.

Although unremembered traumas may be impacting you today, you *can* use EFT to heal from events that you don't recall. Here's an example from my practice.

Theresa, Thomas, and cold fish

Theresa and Thomas came to work with me after they'd been together for two years. They were obviously very much in love and were planning to get married, but difficulties in the bedroom were making them question whether they were meant to be together. They were seeing a couples' therapist, but they also wanted to see if EFT could help.

"When we were dating, sex was fantastic," said Thomas. "Theresa wanted me 24/7. We just had fun together. I had experienced a breakup shortly before we met and wasn't looking for another relationship. But in a matter of a few months, I realized that Theresa was ideal for me, and I asked her to move in. I was falling deeply in love with her, and told her as much. That's when the problem began."

"What problem?" I asked. "Can you describe it to me?"

"Theresa became a cold fish in bed," Thomas said. "She'd just lie there staring up at the ceiling. She wouldn't look at me, touch me, or kiss me at all." At this point, Thomas was visibly upset, so we tapped on his feelings of sadness and hopelessness. While Thomas tapped, I asked Theresa to tap along–a technique known as Borrowing Benefits.

After the work with Thomas was complete, I asked Theresa how she was feeling, and she said she felt sick to her stomach. In EFT, when emotional issues aren't clear, or if practitioners suspect trauma, one way to begin is somatically, which means addressing the physical sensations that present themselves.

I asked Theresa exactly where she felt sick, and if the feeling had weight, texture, or size. We spent considerable time working in this way, using only the bodily sensations that she described in detail as a guide. The sick feeling in her stomach turned into a tight clenching in her chest, and then to a more defused warmth in her throat. It was at that point that Theresa looked at me and said she knew what the problem was.

As a child, Theresa lived next door to a trusted family friend whom her parents thought of as a son. When she was nine, that neighbor sexually abused her. We tapped for several minutes on the shock of remembering this incident and closed by doing a number of additional rounds of tapping on the feelings in her body. Theresa was comfortable waiting until another session to delve into the issue further, and I asked her to talk to her therapist about the discovery we made.

Sexual abuse at the hands of a person that Theresa and her family trusted caused a sense of incongruity, betrayal, and fear that led her to unconsciously "check out" of her body when she was with Thomas. In Theresa's case, sex with people she barely knew seemed safer than sex with Thomas. Her family trusted her abuser, and it was with her trusted beloved that she dissociated.

Theresa and Thomas continued to work with me and with their therapist on healing the trauma and its impact on their relationship. They now enjoy connected, passionate, and intimate lovemaking as a married couple.

Helping your body reveal its secrets

If you need help finding the emotional causes of a physical condition, tune in to what your body is feeling, and follow the procedure in Chapter 10. As was the case with Theresa, following where the pain leads in your body—and tapping on that–may free you to remember the event that's at the root of your condition. Then you can tap on and clear the cause.

CHAPTER 15
WHAT'S THE PAST GOT TO DO WITH IT?

Have you ever wondered why therapists ask so many questions about childhood? It turns out that the most important time in our lives, in terms of building and formulating beliefs, is the first six years. The human brain emits five different types of brain waves–*delta, theta, alpha, beta,* and *gamma*–each associated with a different state. Before the age of six, children spend the majority of their waking lives in *theta* and *delta* states, in which the brain is exceptionally receptive and impressionable. In fact, those are the states that hypnotists cultivate, because it makes their subjects more suggestible. (Lipton, 2008) Because children at that age aren't capable of critical thinking, they can't evaluate the beliefs they form, and therefore sometimes draw erroneous conclusions.

Here's an example of an erroneous conclusion of my own, one that I drew early in life. My family exiled from Cuba when I was three-and-a-half years old. We left with only the clothes we were wearing and started life in a new country where we didn't speak the language. Eighteen months after we arrived, my brother was born.

My father was consumed by his efforts to support us and held three jobs at one point. He experienced a lot of stress as a result, and there were days when my brother and I added to it. Sometimes, Dad got angry and yelled at us, and when that happened, I coped by withdrawing, trying to ignore it, and acting as if my feathers were completely unruffled. It worked! I survived, grew up, left home, and unconsciously attracted romantic partners who were stressed, angry, and yelled a lot.

The partner with whom I lasted the longest resembled my father as he was during my early childhood. I retained the coping strategy that had worked for me all my life, and whenever there was conflict, I checked out, couldn't stay present, and sometimes literally got up and walked away. Confrontation terrified me, and disengaging felt much safer than engaging in those moments.

Years later, I became aware of that pattern as I contemplated how I was able to stay in a sexless marriage for a decade. Naming issues clearly and openly in that relationship felt dangerous. It seemed safer not to speak of the pain I felt about what was happening (or not happening) between us in the bedroom, as well as my dissatisfaction in other areas of our life together.

Looking back, I can see that the way I handled conflict in my marriage relationship was exactly the way I handled it with my father. But the coping strategy that "worked" for me in childhood didn't work at all in adulthood.

Through EFT, you can "rewire" erroneous connections that you made in the past and free yourself to behave in ways that serve you better today. I used EFT to clear my fear of confrontation, fear of getting yelled at, and fear of getting into trouble. Eventually, I was able to voice what wasn't working for me in our relationship, but by then, it was too far gone to salvage. My partner and I decided to split up.

The next issue I faced was overcoming my family of origin's ironclad commitment to staying together, no matter the cost, which I had also internalized as a child. I faced the feelings of failure that most people encounter when a long-term relationship ends, particularly one in which children are involved, and tapped my way through all of it.

I remarried, and am now able to voice what I want, have disagreements, and feel comfortable working through them. I'm now able to model for my children how a healthy relationship works, and they agree, now that they are young adults, that the benefit of a healthier mom and better role model eclipses the pain of my split with their father.

When smoke alarms go off too often

A neighbor recently complained about her smoke alarm, which often goes off while she's preparing meals for her family. She doesn't like having to interrupt what she's doing to go fan the alarm with a dish towel. "I wish they made a voice-activated smoke alarm that turns off when I yell, 'I'm just cooking!'" she said.

To the alarm, smoke is smoke, regardless of the context, and our brains work in much the same way. Danger is danger. Stephen Porges coined the term "neuroception" to describe how our neural circuitry constantly takes in information through our senses and analyzes it in an effort to keep us safe. (Porges, 2004) Like a smoke detector that can perceive smoke before you smell it yourself, neuroception registers danger before you're consciously aware of it. That means your body gets ready to protect you *before* you're conscious of danger.

Humans are tribal, and Porges believes we've learned to subdue defensive behaviors so we can enjoy interdependence and safety in numbers. Social engagement helps us survive, but we can't be socially engaged if our "smoke alarm" keeps going off, and our bodies are constantly poised to fight or flee. Safety is an essential prerequisite to establishing connection, and without it, we can't enjoy intimacy.

If you know that your current or potential partner is trustworthy, yet still find yourself constantly on the alert for danger, you may need to tap on the issues that are causing your smoke alarm to misfire. You can start with a setup statement like, "Even though I feel perpetually on guard, I deeply and completely accept myself..." Then tap on the memories, emotions, and physical sensations that arise.

If your "smoke alarm" is misfiring in your relationship, EFT is a way to turn it off. Here's an example from my practice: Ling came to see me because she was afraid that her partner was going to leave her. "I'm terrified that he's cheating on me," she said. Her fear took the form of intense jealousy if her partner didn't call several times a day or "seemed distant." Whenever those things happened, her first thought was, "He's leaving me." Her fear had become so intense that she felt jealous about her partner's conversations with co-workers and resented the time he spent with his daughter.

Ling knew that as she was actually sabotaging her relationship. This had happened with previous boyfriends, and her mistrust (checking cell phone records, spying from her car, looking through emails and bills) had driven her former husband away.

We started by tapping on recent occasions when Ling felt overwhelmed by jealousy. Next, we focused on her previous relationships. Once she saw EFT working, and she began to feel less intense about her current situation, we focused on where her jealousy originated.

Ling had been raised in the country in a lovely village by the sea, where she spent her days playing with cousins and friends. That abruptly ended when her parents got divorced. Ling's mother was then forced to go work in a foreign country to make money, so she sent Ling to live with her great aunt. For a number of years, Ling's great aunt neglected her and made it clear that she was only caring for Ling as a favor to her mother. Meanwhile, Ling's mother established herself in her new country, got remarried, and had several children with her new husband. Then she sent for Ling.

"My feeling was that of jealously and pain," she said. "My new siblings had been enjoying the comfort and love of my mother, while I was abandoned thousands of miles away." We worked on Ling's feelings of abandonment and jealousy. As Ling processed the painful memories about her family, she also naturally let go of her possessiveness around her partner. Her jealousy ended as if by magic, and she and her partner married less than six months later.

Ling's story is another example of a "smoke alarm," sensitized by abandonment in childhood, that later went off in a context in which it was destructive.

The impact of adverse childhood experiences (ACEs)

In the mid-1980s, Vincent Felitti accidentally made a connection between childhood trauma and adult health. A physician, Felitti was working at the Kaiser Permanente obesity clinic, and though many patients were losing significant amounts of weight, he was puzzled by the numbers of successful patients who dropped out of the program. He wondered why patients fled their own success.

Felitti interviewed many of them to determine why they dropped out, and in those interviews he asked additional questions about their medical histories, including their sexual histories. When interviewing one young woman, he intended to ask his usual question about how old she was at the time of her first sexual experience. However, he accidentally asked how much she weighed when she first became sexually active. "Forty pounds," the woman said, and started sobbing. She had experienced incest at the hands of her father.

Felitti noted that this was only the second case of incest he'd run into in 24 years of practice. However, within 10 days of asking other patients the same question, he encountered another case, and 186 patients later, he found that 55 percent of them had experienced some form of sexual abuse. It turned out that for these patients, being overweight wasn't the problem, it was what Felitti called the "solution to an unrecognized prior adversity." Their additional weight made them unattractive enough to keep danger at bay; it prevented unwanted sexual attention, making them feel invisible and safe.

Several years later, the Centers for Disease Control joined Felitti in conducting the largest epidemiological study of its kind, involving 18,000 participants. The purpose of the Adverse Childhood Experiences (ACE) study was to determine whether there was a connection between the adverse experiences that people had in childhood and their health when they became adults. Not surprisingly, they discovered there was.

As it relates to sexuality, the results of the study indicate that the higher participants' score on the 10-question ACE test, the more likely they were to:

- Have intercourse by the age of 15

- Get pregnant (or impregnate someone) as
  a teenager

- Be raped as adults

- Have fifty or more sexual partners

- Have a sexually transmitted disease

- Miscarry pregnancies (Felitti, 2003)

Felitti quotes Swiss psychologist and author Alice Miller, who once said, "The truth about childhood is stored up in our bodies and lives in the depths of our souls. Our intellect can be deceived, our feelings can be numbed and manipulated, our perceptions shamed and confused, our bodies tricked with medication, but our soul never forgets. And because we are one, one whole soul in one body, someday our body will present its bill."

If you're reading this book, the chances are good that your body is presenting its bill, and one of the places it's showing up is in your bedroom. Although you can't change your past, you can use EFT to break its hold on your present and future.

Here's an example from my practice: Harriet was raised in an impoverished backwater town in the South that no longer exists. She was one of nine children, and Harriet's mother made her cook and clean as soon as she was able to reach the stove. Harriet's father was an alcoholic, and her parents often got into huge fights, some of which escalated to domestic violence. Harriet felt that the only way to be safe was to leave home as soon as she could.

At the age of 14, Harriet found work in a restaurant in the next town. The proprietors of the restaurant allowed her to stay there, in a storage closet. Harriet was left to her own devices at night, and she soon fell in with a much older man named Theodore. With him, Harriet felt comfort and love that she hadn't felt at home, and without much thought, she had sex with him and got pregnant.

The stigma of out-of-wedlock pregnancy was very real, and young women who found themselves in that position were forced into marriage or sent away to have their illegitimate children in special homes for unwed mothers. If you were poor, fewer options were available. However, Theodore came from money, and when his family found out about the pregnancy, they had a housekeeper take Harriet to an abortionist in the city.

Harriet's adverse childhood experiences culminated in an event that Harriet felt was so shameful that she had never told anyone about it. Together, we worked through the shame of the abortion, as well as her painful early family memories. Harriet left at peace with her past–which is what she'd come to achieve.

CHAPTER 16
HEALING THE
ULTIMATE BETRAYAL

I never knew how prevalent childhood sexual abuse was in our society until I became an EFT practitioner. Clients sought help with all sorts of problems, including things like relationship issues, physical illness, the inability to find meaningful work, and overwhelming fears. Often, the root of the problem turned out to be sexual injury.

In its Adverse Childhood Experiences (ACE) study, the Centers for Disease Control and Prevention found that 24 percent of the adult women they surveyed and 16 percent of men experienced childhood sexual abuse. (Centers for Disease Control and Prevention , 2014)

Child abuse and neglect doesn't usually involve "stranger danger." According to a report by the U.S. Department of Health and Human Services, 91.4 percent of the victims of neglect, physical abuse, and sexual abuse were maltreated by their parents, 12.9 percent by people they knew, and 6.8 percent by a person they didn't know. (This adds up to more than 100 percent because perpetrators are counted each time they're associated with maltreating a child.) (U.S. Department of Health and Human Services , 2013)

According to this report, a perpetrator is "a person who was determined to have caused or knowingly allowed the maltreatment of a child." In my practice, I've found that clients feel betrayed by their abusers, but they feel just as betrayed by those who allowed it to take place, didn't believe it was happening, or allied themselves with the perpetrator instead of with them.

Primary betrayal

Primary perpetrators are those who commit sexual abuse, which the report cited above defines as a "type of maltreatment that refers to the involvement of the child in sexual activity to provide sexual gratification or financial benefit to the perpetrator, including contacts for sexual purposes, molestation, statutory rape, prostitution, pornography, exposure, incest, or other sexually exploitative activities." Although most of this type of maltreatment is perpetrated by adults, 23 percent is perpetrated by people under the age of 18. (Snyder, 2000)

My clients have confirmed the results of the ACE study time and time again: adverse childhood experiences correlate to physical diseases in adulthood. Clients struggling with painful menstruation, uterine and cervical cancer, uterine fibroids, problems conceiving, and difficulty in childbirth have had one thing in common: childhood sexual abuse.

Not surprisingly, the survivors of childhood sexual abuse also have interpersonal issues in common, some of which include:

- Difficulty trusting men

- The inability to be in a relationship

- Avoidance of sex

- Difficulty having sex with intimate partners, but not with virtual strangers

- Great sex until engagement or marriage takes place

- Dissociation (difficulty staying fully present and connected) during sex

- Risky sexual behavior

- Poor judgment when choosing romantic partners

- Sexual fetishes or the compulsion to re-enact their abuse

Many of these clients also share a sense of vulnerability that leave them feeling hypervigilant 24/7.

When I work with a client, the root causes of her specific symptoms are usually unknown to both of us, but they often surface in the course of our work together. Here's an example from my practice: Hilda had been in labor with her first child for about 12 hours when her boyfriend contacted me. In the U.S., birthing is often a timed event, and if a mother doesn't give birth within a certain window of time, her labor may be labeled "failure to progress." This can trigger all sorts of interventions, including a C-section, which was something Hilda wanted very much to avoid. Hilda knew she was at the top of a slippery slope that she didn't want to go down.

One of the things I've noticed in my years of EFT practice is that pain is very much influenced by stress. I've also found that the more afraid clients are, the more pain they feel. We started by tapping on Hilda's fear that she'd have to have a C-section and the stress of having to give birth "on schedule." We also tapped on Hilda's fear of failure around the possibility of not being able to give birth naturally, which was something she desired. Her pain immediately began to dissipate.

I then asked Hilda to describe what her pain felt like. She said it made her feel completely "out of control" and that she couldn't relax because she felt like her body was "betraying her." When I asked Hilda when she'd felt that way before, she said she felt exactly the same sensations when she was 11, and her stepfather sexually abused her.

Through the next hour, we worked cautiously and carefully on one particular memory. By the end of the session, Hilda felt at peace and actually relaxed enough to sleep. When she awoke, her contractions were stronger and closer together, but she was in a lot less pain than she'd been in before. After a brief phone call with her physician, Hilda went to the hospital, where she soon gave birth to a healthy baby girl.

As is the case for many women, the pain she endured in childhood lay buried until it was unearthed while she gave birth to her own child. The pain of childbirth can be a gateway to healing and rebirth for the mother, and that turned out to be true for Hilda.

Secondary betrayal

My clients often feel as betrayed by the adults who turned a blind eye to their abuse as they do by the abusers themselves. Sometimes more so. These secondary perpetrators are adults who ignored signs, failed to protect children, or refused to believe what those children said–even after they became adults.

I've had a number of clients whose psychotherapists suggested that they invite the client's parents to a session, so the client could tell them about their abuse. This took place after a great deal of therapy and was considered the next step on the road to healing. But time after time, these clients' stories were met with disbelief, denial, and comments like, "You're lying." "You must've done something to make that happen." "He was young, are you sure you weren't just playing doctor?" "Father Daniel would never do something like that." "Why couldn't you just behave yourself?" And "You're delusional."

We're led to believe that telling a trusted adult about abuse will make it stop, but some abused children's families reject and disown them. By denying the truth, and getting rid of the "troublemaker," they manage to keep their family and reputation intact. One of my clients was sexually abused by her brother when she was 10, for example. She told her mother, who sent her away to live with relatives. The perpetrator, her mother's favorite child, remained at home.

While filming a documentary in Israel about the use of EFT for trauma, I worked with another client, Ahuva, who is an Orthodox Jew. Ahuva wanted help with her feelings of anger, which was adversely impacting her relationship with her young children. Nothing made Ahuva angrier than Arabs, and much of our conversation centered around that. But every time I tried to get to the source of her anger, a wave of gastrointestinal distress sent her running for the bathroom. We stopped filming each time, but she chose to continue the session.

Finally, when I asked her, "Who are you *really* angry with?" She answered, "My parents! They sent me back to the same school where I'd been sexually abused, even after I told them about it." Ahuva wasn't angry at her abuser. She was angry at her parents, who, knowing about her sexual abuse, deliberately re-exposed her to it. We tapped on her anger toward them.

"As an Orthodox Jewish woman, how OK is it to be angry at your parents?" I asked Ahuva. "It's not OK at all," she said. "I *can't* be angry at them."

Thus, Ahuva directed her anger toward Arabs, which was a culturally acceptable alternative. As Ahuva made peace with her past through EFT, she became less triggered and felt less anger when she was with her children.

EFT offers a path to healing, but do not travel alone

If you've experience the ultimate betrayal of childhood sexual abuse, EFT can help, but don't attempt to work alone. Based on attendance at my workshops, I know that a growing number of licensed psychotherapists are learning EFT, and they have more training in trauma than most EFT practitioners.

There is hope.

CHAPTER 17

RECOVERING FROM ABANDONMENT AND NEGLECT

What do Harry Potter, Neville Longbottom, and Lord Voldemort have in common? All three were abandoned: Harry when his parents died, Neville when his parents went mad, and Voldemort when his father left his pregnant mother, who died after Voldemort was born.

Writers seem to think that abandonment makes for a good origin story, but it doesn't seem one bit entertaining when it happens to you. The impact of abandonment is far-reaching and can adversely affect relationships throughout life. People who were abandoned as children often feel as if they're unworthy of commitment, and as soon as someone *does* commit, they feel anxious about that person leaving. It can also be difficult for people who were abandoned as children to form attachments to or trust others.

Here's an example from my practice: Susan contacted me from Europe, saying that she wanted desperately to get rid of the absolute terror she felt at the thought of her boyfriend leaving her. We tapped on that fear, and its intensity dropped from a nine to a two. At that point, Susan's attention shifted to the pain of the divorce she'd gone through a few years earlier. We tapped on scenes related to being abandoned by her ex-husband and, by the end of that session, she felt no fear at all when I asked her to imagine her boyfriend leaving. She didn't feel any intensity related to her ex-husband's departure either.

During the next session, I asked Susan if other men had left her before her marriage failed. The fact that she'd said, "They always leave me," during a round of tapping was my clue. When statements include "always" or "never," I suspect that clients are uncovering a core issue. Susan didn't know where her belief that people always leave her originated, so I had her use a global setup statement: "Even though people always leave me..." and midway through that round of tapping, she excitedly burst out, "I know where this started!"

Susan was born to a teenaged mother who left her to be raised by her grandparents, but who drifted in and out of Susan's life throughout her childhood. The pattern of becoming attached to her mother, only to have her leave, was established in the early years of Susan's life, which is when children build the foundation of their worldview.

We spent the next two sessions working through some of the most painful scenes from Susan's childhood. By the end of the fourth session, she felt a tremendous sense of freedom from fears and anxiety that had plagued her for her entire life.

Two weeks after our final session, I received an email from Susan that had only a picture of a bouquet of flowers attached to it. I wrote back, thanking her for the photograph, and she encouraged me to zoom in on the bouquet. When I did, I was delighted to see that there was an engagement ring in the center of it. Her boyfriend hadn't left. He'd proposed!

If you're consumed by fears that seem to have no basis in your current situation, it's usually a tip-off that you're dealing with older, core issues. Pay attention when the words "always" and "never" come up while you're tapping. They'll lead to the original wound and give you the opportunity to heal it.

Neglect

At first glance, neglect seems less damaging than abuse. After all, it doesn't *hurt* the way being physically abused does, right? *Wrong*. Neglect means that a child's basic human needs aren't being met, including essentials like food, clothing, shelter, medical care, supervision, protection, education, and nurturing. Hunger hurts. Cold hurts. Injuries resulting from inadequate supervision or protection hurt and sometimes kill.

For every case of child abuse in the U.S., there are three cases of neglect. (U.S. Department of Health and Human Services, 2016) Neglect can adversely impact psychological health, brain development, and relational skills, and can also contribute to risky behaviors.

Here's how neglect affected one of my clients. When Tracy came to see me, she said that her husband had insisted she seek help, or he would "think about ending it." This brought up a lot of emotion in Tracy, so we tapped on that for a while.

When we were able to continue, Tracy said the trouble was her "workaholism." She had a demanding job, but she continually added to her already-heavy workload by taking over failed projects at her company. She felt that if she didn't, the company would fail, "They need me, and if they go under, I'll be out of a job," she said. "Nobody can do what I do there. I'm the most responsible person they've got."

We tapped on her fear of losing her job, as well as her fear of losing her marriage. Both were highly emotionally charged for Tracy. There were several times where we veered off into other areas, such as parenting, but the underlying theme was always the same: "I have to be responsible." During her third session, I asked Tracy where she picked up the theme of responsibility in her life, and she immediately said that it was related to her childhood.

When Tracy was seven and her brother was six, their parents got divorced. Her mother had been the classic stay-at-home "June Cleaver" type of mom until that point, and she had trouble living with the stigma of being the first divorcee in her town. After the divorce, Tracy's mother retreated to her bedroom for long stretches of time, and Tracy remembers seeing many bottles of medicine on her bedside table. Tracy's father tried several times to intervene, but gave up, got remarried, and started a new family not long after the divorce.

Tracy remembers piles of garbage everywhere in her home, the electricity being shut off due to her mother's failure to pay the bills on time, rotten food in the kitchen, and only dirty clothes for her and her brother to wear. At seven years of age, Tracy realized that she needed to be the one in charge. "It was pretty clear," she said. "Be the grown-up or die." She learned to do all the things her mother had done, and do them well.

Soon after our work together, Tracy took a leave of absence from her job. She was able to relax and enjoy time with her family. While she was out, her company realized that Tracy had been doing too much and hired someone new to assist her. Tracy reports that she is now much better able to say "no," and is free of her burdensome sense of responsibility.

The hedgehog's dilemma

The German philospher Arthur Schopenhauer told a story known as the "Hedgehog's Dilemma." (Schopenhauer, 1851) One winter, a number of hedgehogs sought warmth in each other's company, but pricked each other when they drew too close. They separated, grew cold again, and then renewed their attempt at a huddle. Eventually, they realized that they couldn't be together without hurting each other and kept a safe distance.

Humans are similar. The "quills" we grow as a result of early abuse, neglect, and abandonment help protect us. But they also keep others from drawing near. EFT helps you lose the quills, so you can enjoy the intimacy of a loving relationship.

CHAPTER 18

EFT AND YOUR RELATIONSHIP

Every relationship has its problems. The difference between bad relationships and good ones is that, in good ones, partners solve those problems *together*. The things that disconnect partners outside the bedroom disconnect them inside it.

As I was writing this book, the U.S. Food and Drug Administration approved Addyi®, the first prescription drug designed to increase women's libido. It's targeted at women who suffer from hypoactive sexual desire disorder (Pollack, 2015).

Now, I'm not a scientist, but in my experience, an absence of sexual desire never happens in a vacuum. In 1992, John Gottman and his colleagues published research that showed they were able to predict whether a couple would divorce with 93.6 percent accuracy. (Buehlman, Gottman, & Katz, 1992) Since then, Gottman has done more research into what makes some relationships succeed and others fail, and a sure sign of trouble is the appearance of one or more of the "four horsemen of the apocalypse." These include criticism, contempt, defensiveness, and stonewalling, and will lead to the end of your relationship if behaviors don't change. (Lisitsa, 2013)

I don't know about you, but if there were apocalyptic horsemen galloping around my bedroom, I wouldn't feel a lot of desire, even *with* medication. Increasing desire by eliminating "horsemen" makes a lot more sense to me than attempting to do it with a prescription.

Money

According to a study titled "Examining the Relationship Between Financial Issues and Divorce," arguments about money are the top predictor of divorce. (Dew, Britt, & Huston, 2012) Harmony around financial issues translates into harmony in your relationship.

How might financial issues be damaging your relationship? Read through the list of questions below and see if any of them apply to you.

- Are the apocalyptic horsemen of criticism, contempt, defensiveness, or stonewalling trampling through your finances?

- Do you earn more than your partner and/or resent him for not contributing more to family finances?

- Do you earn less than your partner and resent him for earning more?

- Do you and your partner disagree on the things you spend your money on?

- Do you get angry with your partner for spending money on things you haven't agreed on?

- Do you and your partner share a financial vision?

- When there are downturns in your financial situation, do you:

- Blame or attack each other?

- Avoid the problem?

- Work together as a team to turn things around?

- Do you pay your bills together or defer the responsibility of bill-paying to your partner?

- Do you know what your overall financial picture is, or have you delegated that responsibility to your partner?

- Are you in debt?

- Do you harbor any resentments toward your partner for his share of that debt?

- Are you a stay-at-home parent who feels completely dependent on your partner?

- If so, are you resentful about having given up your career to take care of your children?

- If your partner is financially supporting you, do you feel like having sex is one of the ways you "earn your keep?"

Don't overlook the impact that financial issues can have on your relationship. They're worth bringing to light, so you can tap on them.

Like so many of my clients, Celia felt that all the conventional ways of dealing with her relationship issues hadn't worked, so she thought she'd try something "out of the box." In our first session, she said that money issues were at the root of her problems with Roc, her partner. "I don't trust Roc with our money, and yet I feel completely stuck," she said. "I don't know where I'd begin to get the money for a divorce, and I'd end up being responsible for our twenty thousand dollars in debt."

She told me that they had the same fight every week, when she discovered a new golf club, a designer shirt, or a bill for an extravagant lunch. She'd been feeling the lack of money since she'd left her fulltime job in the corporate world and started freelancing, a choice she made so she could care for their three-year-old daughter. Until then, Cecilia had had a successful career and had earned more than $100,000 a year. After a few failed attempts at finding a nanny who she felt comfortable with, Celia decided to leave her job. She didn't expect motherhood to be so challenging, but she felt it was well worth her effort.

Celia felt overwhelmed and stressed, but found herself unable to tell Roc how she felt. That led to the sense that they weren't a couple any longer. Although they loved each other, romantic love felt like an elusive dream. When I asked her about their sex life she answered, "What sex life?

We have sex on our anniversary and our birthdays. That's it."

For the first few sessions, Cecilia and I tapped on her childhood money issues. She'd grown up in a family of six, where money was always in short supply. From the moment she took her first job at age 14, Celia had made a vow that she'd always have money and not feel powerless over it. The fact that she now relied on Roc had brought up those childhood fears. She resented Roc for being frivolous in his spending and realized that she'd been behaving passive-aggressively in and out of the bedroom as a result. (People who are passive-aggressive avoid direct expressions of anger and express it in indirect ways instead.)

Roc had completely supported Cecilia's decision to stay home. The biggest problem for him was the pressure of being the sole breadwinner, which led to passive-aggressive overspending on his part. Because I had already started working with Cecilia on her issues, I referred Roc out to another EFT practitioner. Roc was able to release the burden he felt and began having open conversations with Celia about their overall financial picture. Cecilia began to feel more connected with him as a romantic partner. The fighting stopped, they created a budget that they maintained, and they began to enjoy each other as a romantic couple again.

Parenthood

I'm astonished that *anyone* thinks having a baby could save a relationship. My children were born 18 months apart, and the first five or six years of their childhood was a blur. I juggled the needs of a teething toddler, a hungry baby, and a husband who had to catch the 7:55 a.m. train to work. Days were filled with meals, snacks, differing nap schedules, countless diaper changes, laundry, meal preparation, and appointments.

I felt pressure to do things "right" and feared ruining my kids' childhood if I didn't. While they napped, I studied books on parenting and child development. I felt like it was my responsibility to establish the foundation for the strong, capable, resilient adults that I wanted them to become.

Meal preparation was complicated because of all the foods that my nursing infant was sensitive to and my toddler wouldn't eat. When my partner came home, he expected dinner. By the time I'd prepared it, cleaned up afterward, and wrestled two children to bed, sex was the farthest thing from my mind. I was also beginning to grow resentful about the inequity of our responsibilities around the house and around caring for our kids. Sound familiar?

Most of my clients don't come to me when they're in the midst of that chaos. They come when they realize that they haven't been sexual with their partners in a long time, and they know that they're at a point when they need to heal their marriage or they'll lose it. One client said, "If this is what it's like now, while the kids are still growing up, I'm afraid there'll be nothing left when they leave home and have lives of their own."

Here are some questions that may help you identify parenting issues that are harming your relationship. Use them as inspiration for questions of your own.

- Do the apocalyptic horsemen of criticism, contempt, defensiveness, or stonewalling show up around the subject of child-rearing?

- Do you and your partner disagree on how to raise your children?

- Do you harbor resentments toward your partner because you're the one who usually cares for your children?

- Does a constant state of vigilance to your child(ren)'s needs prevent you from being present to your partner?

- Are you having trouble reconciling your roles as a mother and as a lover?

- Do you feel less attractive in your post-baby body?

- Are you afraid sex might be painful after having given birth?

- Was your birth experience traumatic?

It's easy to lose sight of issues like this in the all-consuming work of parenthood, but if your relationship is important to you, it's essential to bring them to the light of day and tap on them. My own first marriage might have survived if I hadn't waited so long.

As a mother, I was afraid that if I wasn't constantly attentive to the needs of my children, I wasn't being a good mom. I became the "expert" and didn't give my partner an opportunity to develop his own expertise, denying him experience with his children and me time for myself. If I had tapped on that during those years, I would have realized that my needs, as well as those of my partner, were as important as the needs of the children. I would have asked for more help and allowed myself more self-care. Unfortunately, I didn't know how to do EFT at the time.

Physical issues

Illness can be a subconscious form of passive aggression. I've had many clients come to me with candida, migraines, fibroids, recurring urinary tract infections, and all sorts of gynecological issues that gave them a terrific excuse to say "no" to sex.

There are no coincidences when it comes to working on physical problems with EFT, and physical conditions like these can show up before you're even consciously aware of problems in your relationship. If you're suffering from a condition that limits intimacy with your partner, be honest with yourself. Are you *relieved* that it gives you a reason not to have sex? If so, you've definitely found something to tap on!

Amelia came to see me because she'd been dealing with a condition called vulvar vestibulitis syndrome (VVS) for about

10 years. VVS can cause severe vaginal pain during sexual intercourse, pelvic exams, and the insertion of tampons. In Amelia's case, she only experienced pain when she and her husband attempted to have sex. "I feel cut off from the waist down," she said. Amelia had seen a number of doctors, an acupuncturist, and had taken supplements, prescriptions, and over-the-counter medications, but found no relief. Her condition left her feeling hopeless and depressed.

When I asked Amelia when the pain started, she said it began around the time that she and her husband moved, leaving behind their support network. "All I had was Frank, and he wasn't there for me," she said. "It felt like a wall went up between us."

When an issue has been around as long as Amelia's, there's usually more than one contributing factor, and we tapped on a number of things that, together, had caused Amelia's body to reach a tipping point. After working together for three months, Amelia's VVS disappeared for good. Four years later, she and Frank are still together, and the VVS never returned.

Distractions

In a 2013 poll conducted by Harris Interactive, nine percent of American adults admitted that they used their smartphones during sex. Among 18-34 year-olds the number was 20 percent. In the same poll, participants were asked what they couldn't live without, and respondents indicated that they'd rather live without sex than live without Internet access, mobile phones, computers, or televisions. (Harris, 2014)

Now that you we can use smartphones on airplanes, I think "airplane mode" should be renamed "relationship mode." Imagine switching your phone to airplane mode during dinner and for an hour afterward every night, so you can spend time connecting with your partner. What thoughts arise for you when you do? What fears?

They might include:

- I'm afraid I'd miss an important communication from a colleague.

- I'm afraid I might miss an opportunity to have fun with friends.

- I would feel disconnected and out of touch.

- I would fall behind.

Now think of it the other way around. What are the hidden benefits of allowing "device intrusion" into your relationship?

Some to consider are:

- If I didn't have the distraction of my phone, my partner and I would have to confront the fact that we're unhappy.

- Without our phones, my partner and I would have to talk more.

- With my phone, I'm able to keep one foot outside our relationship and easily connect with people other than my partner.

Has your device become more important than your relationship? If so, why? Be honest with yourself and tap on the issues that arise. You'll know you've healed when you can easily set your device to "relationship mode" and focus fully on each other.

Reestablishing connection

Intimacy establishes a virtuous circle. Having sex establishes the connection that makes things easier to talk about, and talking about and resolving issues makes it easier to have sex. Begin your work by tapping on your fear of identifying and talking about relationship issues with your partner. Once your fears are gone, making positive changes will come much more easily.

CHAPTER 19
HEALING THE SEXLESS MARRIAGE

Do you remember the scene from *Gone with the Wind* in which Scarlet tells Rhett that she doesn't want any more children? What she was really saying was, "No more nookie, Rhett." Childbirth could be fatal, and in the days before birth control, men who loved their wives willingly agreed to forego sex to protect them.

Even though we can prevent pregnancy, today, many of us still aren't having sex. Some experts define a sexless marriage as exactly that: zero sex. Others consider a marriage in which couples have sex ten to twelve times a year sexless.

A 2010 study conducted at Indiana University shows that the number of sexless marriages double every decade through people's thirties, forties, and fifties. By their sixties, a third of couples are having no sex whatsoever, and by their seventies, more than half have none. (Reece, Herbenick, Schick, Sanders, Dodge, & Fortenberry, 2010)

Age	Percent of married men reporting no sex at all the previous year	Percent of married men reporting sex a few times to monthly
30 - 39	4.5	15.6
40 - 49	9.1	16.2
50 - 59	20.6	25.0
60 - 69	33.9	21.2
70+	54.2	24.2

What causes a sexless marriage? Left unaddressed, the issues described in the previous chapters can lead to bad sex, less sex, or no sex. Couples who don't have sex experience weaker immune systems, higher blood pressure, greater risk of heart attacks, more pain, more trouble sleeping, and more stress than couples who do. They also have lower libidos. (Mayer Robinson) What's *not* happening in your bedroom is wide-reaching and can affect every part of your life.

After working on big issues, many of my clients barely recognize the person they used to be. That's exactly how I feel when I look back at who I was in my own 10-year sexless marriage. I thought I was one of those women who just didn't want sex, I was okay with not having it, it wasn't on my mind, and I didn't consider it important. I told myself that my relationship had more positive attributes than sex, and that I was okay with it.

Then I became an EFT practitioner, and one person after another, week after week, came to me with problems around being in a sexless relationship. One day, after three people came to me with that problem, I put my hands in the air and said, "Okay, I get it! I don't need to be hit over the head with this again. I'll take a look at it." I did a lot of tapping on just coming to terms with *looking* at it.

Through tapping, I realized that the relationship I was in wasn't going to fulfill or satisfy me. It had kept me stuck, and my decision to stay in it was based on a lot of fears. Tapping gave me the clarity that I needed to move on without resentment or fear. (That doesn't mean tapping leads to divorce. It just led *me* there. I've had many clients who healed their issues and began enjoying sex in their relationships again.)

Tapping helped me reconnect with my sexual self, and I'm more sexually active in my fifties than I was in my twenties. I know now that sex can be energizing when I'm tired, can get rid of a headache when I have one, and can make me feel calm and relaxed when I'm feeling stressed out. I find it more fulfilling than I did when I was younger, and it keeps the bond between my second husband and me strong.

I love Carl Jung's quote, "One doesn't become enlightened by imagining figures of light, but by making the darkness conscious." The greatest pain can become a major strength in your life when you bring it to the light of day. Now, I realize that it was my destiny to help others with this issue, but first I had to heal myself.

In my experience, absence of desire always has emotional components to it. When I address those with my clients, desire comes back, if it was there at the beginning. Even clients who experienced betrayals such as infidelity have had desire for their partners return after tapping.

If you're struggling with a sexless marriage, start tapping on your fear of talking about it with your partner. That will begin to change the dynamics. Then tap on the specific relationships challenges that you have now, or have had in the past, that could be contributing to what's not happening in the bedroom.

CHAPTER 20
OVERCOMING THE PAIN OF INFIDELITY

While I was writing this book, the Canadian website Ashley Madison, which is devoted to facilitating affairs among people who are married or in committed relationships, was hacked. The hackers made the personal information of more than 30 million users public. (Newitz, 2015)

Now, only a fraction of the people who are "in the market" for an affair would actually register on ashleymadison. com, but research—and many tearful clients—attest to how common affairs are. There's no greater sense of betrayal and pain than discovering that your partner is cheating.

Although it seems impossible to heal broken trust, EFT can help. Bernadette came to see me because she wanted help deciding whether to stay with her husband. She told me that she didn't think she could ever forgive him for having an affair and reported that she and her husband hadn't slept in the same bed since she'd discovered it. I expected her to say that the affair had happened recently, but it had taken place more than five years earlier.

The two of them had gone through marriage counseling and worked on many of the ways they had disconnected prior to the affair, but the lingering visceral sense of betrayal was still present for Bernadette. "I just can't imagine having him inside me after he's been inside another woman," she said.

I started by doing some tapping on her general anxiety and fear of talking about this. Next, we worked on her fear of never being able to get over it. These are just some of the ways that you can take the intensity off an event and settle even before addressing the event directly. At this point, Bernadette was relaxed and ready to tap on what had happened.

One night, Bernadette returned earlier than expected from a business trip and walked in on her husband having sex with a neighbor—someone she had considered a friend. The things that were most hurtful to Bernadette had to do with the images of her husband enjoying sex with someone else, as well as the position the two of them were in—a position she felt was particularly intimate. The images were seared in Bernadette's mind. However, within a few minutes of tapping, the scene lost its intensity and she said, "I see it as a movie that I'm watching. I know it happened, and I can see it, but it no longer has a hold on me."

Many months later, Bernadette let me know that she had resumed having a close physically intimate relationship with her husband, and that the last piece of that entire phase of their marriage was finally over.

Rebuilding trust

Trust is your ability to rely on your partner to keep your

agreements. Sometimes, relationships begin with a fresh slate, and partners trust each other from the outset. Other times, betrayals from past relationships, beginning with each partner's parents, form a rocky foundation that has to be healed before a healthy relationship can be built.

Every relationship has problems, and if you've been with someone long enough, trust of one sort or another will be broken. "How could you forget the car payment? A late payment damages our credit rating and could wreck our chances of qualifying for a mortgage!" Honestly, I wish couples would write this kind of thing into their wedding vows. When partners are committed to working through problems *together*, they come out stronger on the other side.

Although trust might be broken, you can always have *faith* in your commitment to working through whatever problems come your way as a team. You build a "trust bank" by tackling issues as they arise together. The more problems you tackle, the more trust you build.

The fork in the road

If you're dealing with infidelity in your relationship, you're probably wondering if it can survive betrayal. I'm not invested in whether you to stay or go, but I *am* invested in you being true to yourself. That can be especially difficult when your reputation, finances, children, home, family, and community are all entangled with those of your partner. The more entangled you are, the more appealing staying becomes, and the more terrifying striking out on your own seems. But is staying being true to yourself?

When I ask clients whose partners have been unfaithful, "Did you suspect?" They say yes nine times out of ten. It's rare that people had no idea. Usually, some sort of catalyst makes people wake up and reevaluate their lives. Catalysts have included a milestone birthday, accident, illness, the death of a loved one, a "surprise" STD, or a double-betrayal, such as an affair between a spouse and an extended family member or a good friend.

If you're at a fork in the road and aren't sure which direction to take, EFT can help you gain clarity. You can use some of the following ideas to create setup statements for tapping (you'll find more information about how to create setup statements in Chapter 8):

- I should have known.

- I feel like a fool.

- I feel so gullible.

- I should have trusted my feelings.

- I shouldn't have waited so long.

- My finances, children, and community are connected to this person, and I'm stuck with him.

- I'm a coward.

- I can't trust him.

- I can't trust myself.

- I'm not enough.

- If I had _____, this wouldn't have happened.

- If I were _____, this wouldn't have happened.

- I can never trust again.

What does this betrayal remind me of? When else have I felt this betrayed?

If you need help deciding whether to go or stay, my husband and I have created a self-paced, five-part online course called "When to End It, When to Stay" that uses EFT to help you come to a decision that's right for you. You can find it at whentoendit.com.

Infidelity prevention

One thing I know for sure: Healing is possible. Anytime you weather a storm with someone–be it a colleague, friend, or life partner, you emerge with a sense of greater intimacy, deeper connection, and renewed trust. A relationship just doesn't seem "real" until it withstands a test.

The best "marriage insurance" you can have is to be happy–both personally and in your relationship. EFT helped get me there, and I'm sure it can help you, too.

CHAPTER 21
WHEN "AFFAIRS" AREN'T PHYSICAL

A local osteopath has a mobile over the table that her clients lie on. It's a colorful school of fish, each one hanging on a thread that's tied to a wire, and balanced on the other end of that wire is another fish. The mobile is in constant motion, responding to the tiniest movements of air in the room.

Relationships are like that mobile: beautiful when everything's in balance. You say good-morning, and he greets you with a sleepy hug. He makes dinner while you pay the bills. You walk the dog, and he cleans the litter box. When your focus is on each other, there's a symbiosis and an interdependence that makes you feel strong together. Everything feels balanced.

But when your attention is drawn outside the relationship, things can quickly become unbalanced. Two slippery slopes that people often don't realize they're on, until their relationship is damaged or destroyed, are porn and emotional affairs.

Digital infidelity

There's a big difference between the "old school," print-based porn that teenaged boys used to hide under their mattress and the digital video porn that's ubiquitous on the Internet today. Internet porn can lead to what endocrinologist Frank Beach calls the "Coolidge Effect." The term refers to a (likely apocryphal) story about President Calvin Coolidge and his wife, who were touring a farm separately. Mrs. Coolidge noticed the frequency with which a rooster was mating. She asked how often he did that, and her tour guide said the rooster mated dozens of times a day. "Tell that to the president," she said. When the president was told, he asked whether the rooster mated with the same hen every time. No, the guide said, the hen was different each time. "Tell that to Mrs. Coolidge," the president said. (Dewsbury, 2000)

The rooster was responding to a survival-of-the-fittest instinct to distribute his DNA and leave no hen unfertilized. Had he been in a cage with a single hen, the frequency with which he mated would have plummeted. Like the rooster, humans are wired to respond to novelty, and Internet porn provides plenty of that. Having sex with the same flesh-and-blood partner day after day pales in comparison to the different actors, settings, and sexual acts that Internet porn offers in unending permutations.

"The addictiveness of Internet pornography is not a metaphor," says Norman Doidge, author of *The Brain that Changes Itself.* "Not all addictions are to drugs or alcohol. People can be seriously addicted to gambling, even to running. All addicts show a loss of control of the activity, compulsively seek it out despite negative consequences, develop tolerance so that they need higher and higher levels of stimulation for satisfaction, and experience withdrawal if they can't consummate the addictive act." (Doidge, 2007)

Internet porn can lead to porn-induced erectile dysfunction and can cause people to be less satisfied with their intimate partners. In a study published in the Journal of Applied Social Psychology, researchers found that after consuming pornography, subjects were less satisfied with their partner's physical appearance, sexual curiosity, sexual performance, and affection. Subjects also placed a higher value on sex that took place in the absence of emotional connection. (Zillmann & Bryant, 2006)

My client Tatiana was a beautiful woman who exercised, was diet-conscious, and invested in her appearance. She'd been married to Felix for about ten years when she noticed that the frequency of their love-making had dwindled to less than a quarter of what it had been when they first got married. She suspected another woman, so she checked his computer one day when he was out of town. What she discovered shocked her: he'd been visiting hard core porn sites on the Internet almost daily.

I've helped women tap on the shock of discovering that their partner regularly watches porn more times than I care to recall. After Tatiana discovered porn on Felix's computer, she came in to work on her resistance to having sex with him again. We tapped on the anger and betrayal she felt. "He's having an affair with his screen!" she said. "It's worse than if he'd cheated with a real woman—at least then, I could compete."

After we worked on the shock and trauma of Tatiana's discovery, we tapped on the fact that Felix would be coming home the next day, and she knew she'd have to pretend that everything was fine until their kids went off to bed. At our next appointment, we tapped on Tatiana's sadness that, instead of apologizing for hurting her, Felix got angry that she'd invaded his privacy by looking on his computer.

Felix later apologized, and I sent Tatiana home with the assignment to simply *imagine* having sex with her husband and to note her observations. By this time, it had been six months since they'd had sex. When Tatiana returned, she said she'd been able to identify another reason she felt uncomfortable about being intimate with Felix. She knew her body didn't meet porn-star standards and that she was unable (and unwilling) to do some of the things that apparently turned him on. Real women like Tatiana have imperfect bodies, require foreplay, have body hair, don't necessary enjoy bodily fluids all over their faces, don't orgasm instantaneously, and aren't perpetually aroused.

Tatiana couldn't get the images of her own naked body out of her head. She knew she couldn't hold a candle to Felix's "digital mistresses." We had to tap for several sessions on those images and how they had made her feel.

In the end, Tatiana felt comfortable enough with herself that she and Felix did re-establish a healthy sex life. While she and I were working together, Felix worked with a counselor on unplugging from his computer. It can take months to "disconnect" porn from the pleasure centers of the brain and reconnect with a flesh-and-blood partner. (For more information about this process, I recommend the website yourbrainonporn.com.)

Regardless of the circumstances that clients come to me with, the thing we work on is how it impacts *them*. In Tatiana and Felix's case, we worked on how Felix's porn consumption made *Tatiana* feel. We didn't work to change Felix.

If you find yourself in a similar situation, use EFT on how your circumstance impacts *you* emotionally.

Emotional infidelity

I've heard it said that women need to feel connected to be sexual, and that men need to be sexual to feel connected. The clients in my practice seem to bear that out. Women come to me because their partners have had a physical affair or because they themselves have become involved in an emotional one.

Sissy is an example. She was content with her marriage, had the perfect house in the right neighborhood, a small business as a commercial artist, and a ten-year-old daughter she adored. Her husband was the main breadwinner, and she wasn't looking for anything else in her life. But two things happened that made her reevaluate everything: her mother died, and she met someone new.

Sissy once asked her mother if she was actually happy. "I was taught not to ask those kinds of questions," her mother said. "They'll only lead to discontentment with your own life." The only role Sissy's mom had ever played was that of a mother and grandmother, and as soon as her youngest grandchild turned 13, she passed away.

A few weeks after her mother's memorial service, Sissy went on a spiritual retreat in a country that had always fascinated her. Participants spent part of the time in reflection alone and part of it reflecting with each other. That's when Sissy met Leo, who was everything her husband didn't seem to be: spiritual and truly interested in Sissy's innermost thoughts.

Not long after returning home, Sissy came to see me to work through her feelings about the situation. She hadn't crossed the line by kissing or having sex with Leo, but she felt that the intimacy they'd shared was the equivalent of adultery. We worked on how painful it was for her to be separated from Leo and how much she longed to be with him again now that she was home. We also worked on the chemistry that they had shared and her fantasies about what his kiss or his arms around her would feel like.

Sissy felt guilty about what she'd done to jeopardize her family and marriage. But at the same time, she wondered if she was repeating her mother's pattern and living only for her family and not herself. Was Leo Sissy's only chance at real happiness?

In the end, Sissy decided that she wanted to stay with her husband and to work with him to get out of the relationship slump they'd been in. It turned out that her husband had wonderful qualities that she just hadn't seen. Together, they found creative ways to reignite the passion that had been there when they first met.

EFT helped Tatiana and Sissy make the decision that was right for them. In their case, that meant staying with their partners, but I've had just as many clients in similar situations who decided to end their long-term relationships. EFT didn't sway them in one direction or another. It simply facilitated clarity, and when clients decided to end their relationships, it helped them do that with grace. Rather than running away from their old lives and repeating the same mistakes, EFT helped them heal past wounds, find closure, and move forward with a new life.

CHAPTER 22
YOUR TAPPING TROUBLESHOOTER

One of the most unusual places I've ever been asked to give an EFT demonstration is at a museum in Seattle. It was an art installation on America's DIY (do it yourself) culture, and when I arrived, I discovered that I'd be presenting in a room whose walls were completely covered with monitors, each of which was playing a different how-to-tap video.

"This is my worst nightmare," I said to my husband.

When I learned EFT, there was only one source: Gary Craig, his emofree.com website, his free downloadable instruction manual, and his instructional DVDs. Gary wholeheartedly and enthusiastically made EFT accessible to all in hopes of empowering people to heal themselves. Unfortunately, Gary's generosity had a down side: others took EFT and modified it in countless ways.

I learned EFT in 2005, the year YouTube was invented. As I write, a YouTube search for EFT turns up nearly 260,000 videos, most of which either aren't the original EFT, or which contain cookie-cutter "tap-along" scripts. Although tap-along videos are a good way to learn the EFT tapping points, they aren't usually effective for addressing specific issues. As you'll see later in this chapter, specificity is the key to successful tapping.

These videos and conflicting information on the Internet have led to what Gary calls "the silent sea of discontented EFT experimenters" who tried EFT and concluded that it doesn't work for them. (Craig)

Had I sought help for my issues now, instead of in 2005, I would have been confused and overwhelmed by all the information on the Internet, too. I wouldn't have known where to start or whom to trust, and I would most certainly have been part of that silent sea of discontentment.

But the success I experienced when I began using EFT, and the countless successes I've seen since, makes me confident that EFT works. When it doesn't, I ask my clients and students the following questions.

Are you being specific?

I can't emphasize strongly enough how important it is to be specific when you're doing EFT, and that's why tap-along scripts and videos don't generally work. Whenever you start tapping, you begin a treasure hunt whose object is to find and eliminate the source of your issue. Being specific increases the likelihood that you'll find that X-marks-the-spot place where it all began.

For example, say you're mad at your husband. You could start your setup statement with: "Even though I'm angry at my husband...." Or you could say: "Even though I'm angry at Brian for forgetting our anniversary yesterday...."

The second setup statement is more likely to surface something like: "And he forgot my birthday last year, too." Which is likely to surface something like: "Right after Grandma died, Mom forgot my seventh birthday." And so on. As I've said before, the presenting issue is almost *never* the source of the problem. One memory leads to another, and you keep tapping until you have the "Aha moment" that tells you that you've found the source of the problem. At that point, you'll feel relief and no, or very little, emotional intensity.

Not being specific enough is the most common reason why EFT doesn't work. When clients say EFT isn't working, and I ask what they were tapping on, nine times out of ten, they were tapping on something general instead of something specific.

Are you tapping on something positive instead of something negative?

The second most common reason that EFT doesn't work is when people turn negative statements into positive ones. For example, instead of starting your setup statement with: "Even though I'm angry at Brian for forgetting our anniversary yesterday...." and staying with that honest anger, you might try to reframe it and look on the bright side. For example: "Even though I'm angry at Brian for forgetting our anniversary yesterday, at heart, I know he's a really great guy."

I love the fact that EFT starts with what's true for me. If I feel mad, it's OK to be mad and work from there. Dr. Gabor Mate's excellent book *When the Body Says No* is all about the high physical cost of emotional repression. He likes to quote a line that Woody Allen says in the movie *Manhattan*. "I don't get angry, OK? I have a tendency to internalize. I can't express anger, that's one of the problems I have. I grow a tumor instead."

Emotions will find expression one way or another. You can't heal what you won't allow yourself to feel, and EFT makes it safe to have emotions that you may have been repressing. When you tap on emotions organically, as they arise, a cognitive shift toward the positive naturally takes place. This is far more powerful, authentic, and lasting than a reframe.

Are you scoring emotional intensity?

When you don't score emotional intensity (on a zero-to-ten or low/medium/high scale) with each round of tapping, you don't have the information you need to proceed.

If your score is dropping with each round of tapping, you know EFT is working.

If your score *isn't* dropping, try all the suggestions in this chapter. If none of them make EFT more effective, contact an EFT practitioner.

Are you documenting your experiences?

One of the most fascinating phenomena I've come across in EFT is something called the "apex effect," which is when people start tapping on a specific problem, then, after tapping, claim it was never a problem to begin with.

In one of my workshops, for example, I worked with Heather. She felt an emotional intensity of 10 about something she'd done when her son was a child that he still couldn't forgive her for, even though he was now an adult. The situation was so painful for Heather that she couldn't even talk about it.

After we tapped, I asked her how her son's inability to forgive her made her feel now. Her intensity had gone down to a zero, and she said, "It never really bothered me."

Wait. What happened? Moments before, the problem so overwhelmed Heather that she couldn't speak, and everyone at the workshop had witnessed it. Fortunately, we had a recording of the session, and when we played it back, Heather was in shock. If she hadn't heard that recording, she wouldn't have remembered how painful the situation with her son had been for her.

This is the apex effect in action. Tapping eliminated the intensity of her emotion, but it also seemed to eliminate her memory of that intensity. The memory itself was still there. She could recall having thrown away one of her son's treasured childhood possessions without his knowledge or permission. And she remembered how upset he was. But she didn't remember how upset *she* was, and she maintained that she'd never been upset.

In his book, *Tapping the Healer Within*, EFT forefather Roger Callahan explains the apex effect this way: "The left brain is being presented with something that it cannot understand (rapid success of tapping) and creates an explanation of its own–contrary to what has taken place. These rationalizations become so powerful that they override all critical thinking."

The apex effect is one of many reasons why I encourage you to download and print the free journal template from my website at tapyourpower.net/book and fill it out for each situation you tap on. As the pages pile up, you'll see how far you've come, and, should you experience the apex effect, you'll have evidence that tapping did, indeed work, even if you think it didn't.

Have you addressed underlying medical issues?

EFT is no substitute for medical care, and when clients come to me with physical ailments, "What does your doctor say?" is one of the first questions I ask. I had a client who couldn't lose weight, for example. She'd gone to several doctors with no results. But when we addressed all the emotional contributing factors using EFT, and she *still* couldn't lose weight, I encouraged her to see another doctor. She did, and they discovered that she had a tumor on her pituitary gland.

EFT can complement traditional medical and psychological care, but it's not a replacement for it. Make sure you've addressed underlying medical or psychological conditions before you turn to EFT.

Is there a hidden benefit that prevents you from letting go of the problem?

In Chapter 5, I wrote about the fact that for some people, the advantages of a problem might outweigh the disadvantages. Obvious examples include people who would lose choice parking spots if they regained mobility and lost their handicapped parking status; people on disability who might have to return to a job they hate if they got well; and the classic "Not tonight, dear, I have a headache" excuse that defers unwanted sex.

Few hidden benefits are that obvious. If you find that EFT isn't working for you, be honest with yourself and consider what the advantages of your situation are. What would you have to give up if you got better? Then tap on your fear of losing that.

Are you dehydrated?

I once did a demonstration at an alternative high school and worked on a student whose back pain wouldn't go lower than an eight on a zero-to-ten scale, no matter what we tried. "What have you had to drink today?" I asked. She'd had only one energy drink, and the caffeine in energy drinks causes dehydration. I asked her to go to the water fountain and drink a lot, and sure enough, during our next round of tapping, her pain dropped from an eight to a two.

Make sure you're well-hydrated when you do EFT.

Are you able to see your own problem objectively?

I heard an expression recently that perfectly describes a phenomenon that we all struggle with at times, and that's, "You can't read the label if you're inside the jar." A similar expression that most of us are more familiar with is: "You can't see the forest for the trees."

It's often difficult to get enough distance from your problem to see it clearly. For example, your husband may be driving you crazy, and you might be convinced that *he's* the problem, but you somehow miss the fact that he's behaving exactly the way your father did. Or you might be so caught up in your weight problems that you don't see that it has much more to do with sexual abuse in your past than it does with your diet and exercise.

This is why working with an EFT practitioner can be so helpful. If you've tried everything else in this chapter and still aren't getting results, find someone outside your "jar" who can help you read the label.

CHAPTER 23
GO FORTH AND HEAL

I didn't set out to become a sexpert. But as I worked with more and more people, I became aware of a universal longing for intimacy, soulful connection, and unconditional love. I also realized that passion isn't just something that shows up in the bedroom. Wherever I go, I find myself drawn to people who are passionate about what they do, whether that's designing websites, making espresso, or performing surgery.

Passion is a universal language that applies everywhere—one I hope this book will help you speak. A passionate job candidate is more likely to get hired, a passionate singer will sell more recordings, and a passionate mom is going to raise kids who know they matter in the world.

Over the years, I've seen more than a thousand clients, taught thousands of students, and I still wake up every morning excited about what I do. Thanks to the power of EFT, I've seen troubled relationships stabilize and blossom; people who were afraid to speak find their voices; and women who experienced the freedom that comes with finally loving their own bodies. I've seen people heal from conditions that their doctors gave up on; middle-aged women thrilled to have had their first orgasm; and people who found they can be more present with their loved ones. I've seen people finally break free of deeply entrenched patterns; marriages that ended without baggage that could doom future relationships; and people overcome the obstacles that prevented them from succeeding.

EFT brings those kinds of changes within your reach. It's a tool that you can use for every aspect of the human experience, and now you know how to do it yourself. But you're not alone. If you're tackling issues that you need help with, feel free to get in touch via tapyourpower.net.

WORKS CITED

CHAPTER 2: HOTDOGS OR HAMBURGERS?

Chapman, G. D. (n.d.). *The 5 Love Languages*. Retrieved September 28, 2015, from The 5 Love Languages: http://www.5lovelanguages.com/

Nagoski, E. (2011, March 5). *Beautiful*. Retrieved September 28, 2015, from The Dirty Normal: http://www.thedirtynormal.com/blog/2011/03/05/beautiful/

Marketdata-Enterprises. (2015, January). *The U.S. Weight Loss Market: 2015 Status Report & Forecast*. Retrieved September 28, 2015, from Bharat Book Bureau: https://www.bharatbook.com/healthcare-market-research-reports-467678/healthcare-industry-healthcare-market-research-reports-healthcare-industry-analysis-healthcare-sector1.html

Statista. (n.d.). *Statista*. Retrieved September 28, 2015, from Statistics and facts on the Cosmetic Industry: http://www.statista.com/topics/1008/cosmetics-industry/

ASAPS. (2014, March 20). *The American Society for Aesthetic Plastic Surgery Reports Americans Spent Largest Amount on Cosmetic Surgery Since The Great Recession of 2008*. Retrieved September 28, 2015, from The American Society for Aesthetic Plastic Surgery: http://www.surgery.org/media/news-releases/the-american-society-for-aesthetic-plastic-surgery-reports-americans-spent-largest-amount-on-cosmetic-surger

CHAPTER 3: TAKING MATTERS INTO YOUR OWN HANDS

Maines, R. P. (1999). *The Technology of Orgasm: "Hysteria", the Vibrator, and Women's Sexual Satisfaction*. Baltimore: The Johns Hopkins University Press.

Stern, M. (2012, 4 27). *'Hysteria' and the Long, Strange History of the Vibrator*. Retrieved September 22, 2015, from The Daily Beast: http://www.thedailybeast.com/articles/2012/04/27/hysteria-and-the-long-strange-history-of-the-vibrator-vertical.html

Vineyard, J. (2012, June 1). *How the Vibrator Came Out of the Closet*. Retrieved September 22, 2015, from Ms. Magazine: http://msmagazine.com/blog/2012/06/01/how-the-vibrator-came-out-of-the-closet/

Schwartz, K. (2014, June 5). *It's Still Illegal to Buy Sex Toys in Some Parts of America. One Woman Is Trying to Fix It*. Retrieved September 22, 2015, from Esquire: http://www.esquire.com/news-politics/news/a28913/legal-ban-on-sex-toys/

Kellogg, J. H. (1881). *Plain Facts for Old and Young*. Burlington: Segner & Condit.

Kling, C. (n.d.). *Love Machines: The secret history of a mass-market appliance*. Retrieved September 22, 2015, from Wired Magazine: http://archive.wired.com/wired/archive/7.01/vibrators_pr.html

Kinsey Institute, *Frequently Asked Sexuality Questions to the Kinsey Institute*. (n.d.). Retrieved September 22, 2015, from The Kinsey Institute: http://www.iub.edu/~kinsey/resources/FAQ.html#masturbation

Shpancer, N. (2010, September 29). *The Masturbation Gap: The Pained History of Self-Pleasure*. Retrieved September 22, 2015, from Psychology Today: https://www.psychologytoday.com/blog/insight-therapy/201009/the-masturbation-gap

Kolodny, C., & Genuske, A. (2015, May 18). *The Overdue, Under-Told Story Of The Clitoris*. Retrieved September 22, 2015, from Huffington Post: http://projects.huffingtonpost.com/cliteracy

Your Brain on Porn. (2010, December 4). Retrieved September 22, 2015, from Your Brain on Porn: http://yourbrainonporn.com/reboot_your_brain

CHAPTER 4: WHAT EFT IS AND HOW IT WORKS

Mosher, D. (2007, August 10). *Greatest Mysteries: What Causes Gravity?* Retrieved October 13, 2015, from Live Science: http://www.livescience.com/1770-greatest-mysteries-gravity.html

Ecker, B., Ticic, R., & Hulley, L. (2012). *Unlocking the Emotional Brain: Eliminating Symptoms at Their Roots Using Memory Reconsolidation.* Routledge.

Kircanski, K., Lieberman, M. D., & Craske, M. G. (2012). Feelings Into Words: Contributions of Language to Exposure Therapy. *Psychological Science.* http://www.scn.ucla.edu/pdf/Kircanski(inpress)PsychSci.pdf

Feinstein, D. (2015). How Energy Psychology Changes Deep Emotional Learnings. *The Neuropsychotherapist*, 48. How Energy Psychology Changes Deep Emotional Learnings. *The Neuropsychotherapist*

Epstein, R. (2001). The Prince of Reason. *Psychology Today*, 72. https://www.psychologytoday.com/articles/200101/the-prince-reason

Ellis, A., & Grieger, R., (1977). *RET: Handbook of Rational-Emotive Therapy.* Springer Publishing Company

Swingle, P. G., Pulos, L. D., & Swingle, M. K. (2005). Neurophysiological Indicators of EFT Treatment of Post-Traumatic Stress. *Journal of Subtle Energies & Energy Medicine*, 75-86. http://journals.sfu.ca/seemj/index.php/seemj/article/viewFile/377/339

Diepold, J. H., & Goldstein, D. (2008). Thought Field Therapy and qEEG Changes in the Treatment of Trauma: A Case Study. *Traumatology*, 85—93.

Hui, K. K., Liu, J., Makris, N., Gollub, R. L., Chen, A. J., Moore, C. I., et al. (2000). Acupuncture modulates the limbic system and subcortical gray structures of the human brain: Evidence from fMRI studies in normal subjects. *Human Brain Mapping*, 13-25.

Church, D., Yount, G., & Brooks, A. (2012). The Effect of Emotional Freedom Technique (EFT) on Stress Biochemistry: A Randomized Controlled Trial. *Journal of Nervous and Mental Disease*, 200(10), 891–896.

CHAPTER 10: OUCH! OVERCOMING PHYSICAL PAIN OR DISCOMFORT

Craig, G. (n.d.). *Chasing the Pain - Deeper EFT Relief*. Retrieved July 14, 2015, from The Home of Gold Standard EFT™ (Emotional Freedom Techniques): http://www.emofree.com/eft-tutorial/tapping-tools/pain-relief.html

CHAPTER 11: HEALING YOUR HEART— OVERCOMING EMOTIONAL PAIN

Statistic Brain Research Institute. (2014, July 8). *Hair Loss Statistics*. Retrieved July 14, 2015, from Statistic Brain Research Institute: http://www.statisticbrain.com/hair-loss-statistics/

Greer, S., & Morris, T. (1975). Psychological attributes of women who develop breast cancer: A controlled study. *Journal of Psychosomatic Research 19*, 147–153.

CHAPTER 14: THE MIND-BODY CONNECTION

Mehta, N. (2011). Mind-body Dualism: A critique from a Health Perspective. *Mensa Sana Monographs*, 202-209.

Carlson, L. E., Beattie, T. L., Giese-Davis, J., Faris, P., Tamagawa, R., Fick, L. J., et al. (2015). Mindfulness-based cancer recovery and supportive-expressive therapy maintain telomere length relative to controls in distressed breast cancer survivors. *Cancer*, 476–484.

CHAPTER 15: WHAT'S THE PAST GOT TO DO WITH IT?

Bruce H. Lipton, P. (2008). The Power of the Mind. *New Dawn Magazine No. 106*. http://www.newdawnmagazine.com/articles/the-power-of-the-mind

Porges, S. (2004, May). Neuroception: A Subconscious System for Detecting Threats and Safety. *Zero to Three Magazine*, pp. 20-24.

Felitti, V. J. (2003, September). *The Relationship of Adverse Childhood*

Experiences to Adult Health Status with Vincent J. Felitti. Retrieved July 27, 2015, from YouTube (Presented by the Primary Children's Center for Safe and Healthy Families and the Division of Child Protection and Family Health, of the Pediatrics Department at the University of Utah): https://youtu.be/Me07G3Erbw8

CHAPTER 16: HEALING THE ULTIMATE BETRAYAL

Centers for Disease Control and Prevention. (2014, May 13). *Prevalence of Individual Adverse Childhood Experiences*. Retrieved August 4, 2015, from Centers for Disease Control and Prevention: http://www.cdc.gov/violenceprevention/acestudy/prevalence.html

U.S. Department of Health and Human Services. (2013). *Child Maltreatment*. 2013: U.S. Department of Health and Human Services.

Snyder, H. N. (2000). *Sexual Assault of Young Children as Reported to Law Enforcement: Victim, Incident, and Offender Characteristics*. Pittsburg: National Center for Juvenile Justice.

CHAPTER 17: RECOVERING FROM ABANDONMENT AND NEGLECT

U.S. Department of Health and Human Services. (2016). *Child Maltreatment 2013*. Washington, D.C.: U.S. Department of Health and Human Services.

Schopenhauer, A. (1851). *Parerga and Paralipomena*. Berlin: Druck und Verlag von U. W. Hahn.

CHAPTER 18: EFT AND YOUR RELATIONSHIP

Pollack, A. (2015, August 18). *F.D.A. Approves Addyi, a Libido Pill for Women*. Retrieved August 23, 2015, from The New York Times: http://www.nytimes.com/2015/08/19/business/fda-approval-addyi-female-viagra.html

Buehlman, K. T., Gottman, J. M., & Katz, L. F. (1992). How a couple views their past predicts their future: Predicting divorce from an oral history interview. *Journal of Family Psychology*, 295-318.

Lisitsa, E. (2013, April 22). *The Four Horsemen*. Retrieved August 23, 2015, from The Gottman Relationship Blog: http://www.gottmanblog.com/four-horsemen/2014/10/29/the-four-horsemen-introduction

Dew, J., Britt, S., & Huston, S. H. (2012). Examining the Relationship Between Financial Issues and Divorce. *Family Relations*, 615–628.

Harris, I. (2014, January 29). *ITDMs' Enthusiasm for Technology Comes with a Cost*. Retrieved August 24, 2015, from Harris Interactive: http://www.harrisinteractive.com/NewsRoom/HarrisPolls/tabid/447/ctl/ReadCustom%20Default/mid/1508/ArticleId/1373/Default.aspx

CHAPTER 19: HEALING THE SEXLESS MARRIAGE

Reece, M., Herbenick, D., Schick, V., Sanders, S., Dodge, B., & Fortenberry, D. (2010). Findings from the National Survey of Sexual Health and Behavior (NSSHB), Center for Sexual Health Promotion. *Journal of Sexual Medicine*, 243–245.

Mayer Robinson, K. (n.d.). *10 Surprising Health Benefits of Sex: The perks of sex extend well beyond the bedroom*. Retrieved August 25, 2015, from webmd.com: http://www.webmd.com/sex-relationships/guide/sex-and-health

CHAPTER 20: OVERCOMING THE PAIN OF INFIDELITY

Newitz, A. (2015, August 26). *Almost None of the Women in the Ashley Madison Database Ever Used the Site*. Retrieved August 31, 2015, from Gizmodo.com: http://gizmodo.com/almost-none-of-the-women-in-the-ashley-madison-database-1725558944

CHAPTER 21: WHEN "AFFAIRS" AREN'T PHYSICAL

Dewsbury, D. A. (2000). "Frank A. Beach, Master Teacher". In G. A. Kimble, & M. Wertheimer, *Portraits of Pioneers in Psychology, Volume 4*. Washington, D.C.: American Psychological Association.

Doidge, N. (2007). *The Brain That Changes Itself: Stories of Personal Triumph from the Frontiers of Brain*. Penguin.

Zillmann, D., & Bryant, J. (2006). Pornography's Impact on Sexual Satisfaction. *Journal of Applied Social Psychology*, 438–453.

CHAPTER 22: YOUR TAPPINGTROUBLESHOOTER

Craig, G. (n.d.). *The EFT Silent Sea of Disappointed People*. Retrieved September 14, 2015, from The Home of Gold Standard EFT™: http://www.emofree.com/eft-tapping-articles/popular/eft-tapping-silent-sea.html? highlight=WyJzZWEiLCJzZWFzIl0=

ACKNOWLEDGEMENTS

I'm eternally grateful to my parents, who model what true physical closeness is after 50 years of marriage; to my children, whose love stirred in me the fire to heal myself, so I could carry my parents' legacy forward; to my darling Craig, who took care of hundreds of daily minutiae and nurtured me both physically and emotionally, so that this book could come to fruition; to Gary Craig, who has transformed millions of lives, including my own, through EFT; to the many women I've coached who had the courage to face their deepest fears and allow me the humble honor of witnessing their sacred transformation; and to Petra Martin, who worked tirelessly to birth this book.

ABOUT THE AUTHOR

Alina Frank first witnessed the mind's ability to facilitate physical healing while practicing as a postpartum doula. Seven years later, she discovered EFT, which she used to eliminate all symptoms of a serious illness and to radically improve her life circumstances. Based on her personal success with EFT, Alina established a private EFT practice and received her certification from EFT founder Gary Craig in 2006. In 2007, she received trauma-specific EFT training from Rabbi Legomsky, director of Israel Trauma Care. Alina became certified in Matrix Reimprinting in 2010 and became a Matrix Reimprinting trainer the following year. She earned her master life coach certification in 2012.

Since 2009, Alina has been consistently rated one of the top EFT practitioners in the U.S. After a number of years in private practice, she wanted to share EFT with more people than she could serve one-on-one, so she became a trainer for several EFT organizations. Together with her husband Craig Weiner, D.C., Alina conducts EFT and Matrix Reimprinting trainings throughout the United States, Canada, Mexico, and Europe.

Alina is the founder and current organizer of the annual Northwest EFT Tappers Gathering and the co-founder of the Matrix Reimprinting Online Summit. She offers free EFT to emergency responders through a nonprofit called Whidbey CareNet, and is a presenter for the Warriors Wellness Project's Trauma Tune-Up. Her work has been published in the *EFT Clinical Handbook* and a number of other books on EFT.

difference press

Difference Press offers solopreneurs, including life coaches, healers, consultants, and community leaders, a comprehensive solution to get their books written, published, and promoted. A boutique-style alternative to self-publishing, Difference Press boasts a fair and easy-to-understand profit structure, low-priced author copies, and author-friendly contract terms. Its founder, Dr. Angela Lauria, has been bringing to life the literary ventures of hundreds of authors-in-transformation since 1994.

LET'S START A MOVEMENT WITH YOUR MESSAGE

You've seen other people make a difference with a book. Now it's your turn. If you are ready to stop watching and start taking massive action. Reach out.

"Yes, I'm ready!"

In a market where hundreds of thousands books are published every year and are never heard from again, all participants of The Author Incubator have bestsellers that are actively changing lives and making a difference.

In less than two years we've created over 100 bestselling books in a row, 90% from first-time authors. As a result, our regular book programs are selling out in advance and we are selecting only the highest quality and highest potential applicants for our future programs.

Our program doesn't just teach you how to write a book—our team of coaches, developmental editors, copy editors, art directors, and marketing experts incubate you from book idea to published bestseller, ensuring that the book you create can actually make a difference in the world. We only work with the people who will use their book to get out there and make that difference.

If you have life-or world-changing ideas or services, a servant's heart, and the willingness to do what it REALLY takes to make a difference in the world with your book, go to http://theAuthorIncubator.com/apply to complete an application for the program today.

Better Videos: Stand out. Be Seen. Create Clients.

by Rachel Dunn

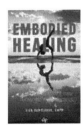

Embodied Healing: Using Yoga to Recover from Trauma and Extreme Stress

by Lisa Danylchuk

Evolve Your Life: Rethink Your Biggest Picture Through Conscious Evolution

by Sheila Cash

Growing Your Separate Ways: 8 Straight Steps to Separating with the Same Intention of Love and Respect You Had...

by Leah Ruppel

How to Want Sex Again: Rekindling Passion with EFT

by Alina Frank

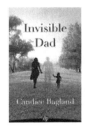

Invisible Dad: How to Heal as a Fatherless Daughter

by Candice Ragland

Not Your Average 5K: A Practical 8-Week Training Plan for Beginning Runners

by Jill Angie

The Cancer Whisperer: How to Let Cancer Heal Your Life

by Sophie Sabbage

*The Unfair Affair:
How to Strengthen
and Save Your
Marriage, or Move
on with Confidence,
After Infidelity*

by Wendy Kay

*Untame Yourself:
Reconnect to the
Lost Art, Power
and Freedom of
Being a Woman*

by Elizabeth DiAlto

*Unveiling Lyme
Disease: Is
This What's
Behind Your
Chronic Illness?*

by Lisa Dennys

*Waking Up With
Dogs: Beginning
at the End*

by Melissa Courtney

*Whoops! I Forgot
To Achieve My
Potential: Create
Your Very Own
Personal Change
Management
Strategy to Get the...*

by Maggie Huffman

*Personal Finance
That Doesn't Suck: A
5-step Guide to Quit
Budgeting, Start
Wealth Building and
Get the Most from...*

by Mindy Crary

*Good Baby, Bad
Sleeper: Discover
Your Child's Sleep
Personality To
Finally Get the
Sleep You Need*

by Stephanie
Hope Dodd

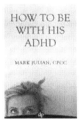

*How You Can Be
with His ADHD:
What You Can
Do To Rescue Your
Relationship When
Your Partner Has
Adult ADHD*

by Mark Julian

Made in the USA
Middletown, DE
11 March 2016